THE IMPACT OF
AKIRA

The Impact of Akira: A Manga [R]evolution
by Rémi Lopez
published by Third Éditions
10 rue des Arts, 31000 Toulouse
contact@thirdeditions.com
www.thirdeditions.com

Follow us: 🐦 @ThirdEditions – f Facebook.com/ThirdEditions
📷 Third Éditions

Publishing Directors: Nicolas Courcier and Mehdi El Kanafi
Publishing Assistants: Ken Bruno, Ludovic Castro and Damien Mecheri
Text: Rémi Lopez
Proofreaders: Zoé Sofer and Anne-Sophie Guénéguès
Layout: Bruno Provezza
Classic Cover: Guillaume Singelin
First Print Cover: Katsuya Terada
Cover Creation: Frédéric Tomé
Translated from French by Jennifer Ligas, ITC Traductions

This informative work is Third Éditions' tribute to the *Akira* manga series and film. The author
retraces a chapter in the history of the *Akira* manga series and film, identifying the inspirations,
background, and content of these works through original reflection and analysis.

English edition, copyright 2020, Third Éditions.
All rights reserved.
ISBN 978-2-37784-280-3
Legal submission: November 2020
Printed in the European Union by Grafo.

RÉMI LOPEZ

THE IMPACT OF
AKIRA

A MANGA
[R]EVOLUTION

03.rd ThirD éditions

For Lou S.

Table of Contents

THE IMPACT OF
AKIRA

A MANGA
[R]EVOLUTION

1.0: Preface

EFYING the orders of an authority they prefer to mock, the motorcycle gang and their young, charismatic leader Kaneda set off to admire the alarming crater that launched World War III. This scar of history is as gaping as it is gloomy. The crater is a symbol of death but also of rebirth, for next to Kaneda stands a concrete monster twinkling with millions of lights, a new Babylon dubbed Neo-Tokyo. In the turmoil of a nascent civil war, Kaneda and his comrades ride their high-tech motorcycles to the tune of their own despair, finding meaning in self-destructive gratification and gang wars that make their drug-tainted blood boil.

It is widely agreed that *Akira* divided the world of manga into a before and an after. This is true for several reasons. First, because the work of Katsuhiro Otomo—with its incredible detail, realism, and dizzying perspectives—inspired an entire generation of young artists. Second, because *Akira* helped create an international market for manga, and more generally for Japanese animation, by trampling the rest of the world's notion that cartoons are exclusively for children. Finally, because anyone who has read or seen *Akira* does not come out of the experience unscathed. The initiated are shocked, seduced, disgusted, excited, or completely fascinated. So much so, that more than thirty-five years after *Akira*'s first chapter was published in *Young Magazine*, the work's provocative nature continues to exert its influence on generation after generation, from Japan to Hollywood, passing through France, which was one of the first countries to open its arms to manga before becoming its second largest global consumer behind Japan.

The aim of this book is to present *Akira* from an intensely Japanese perspective. We will begin by revisiting the career of Katsuhiro Otomo, whose works prior to *Akira* remain relatively unknown outside of his archipelago. We will attempt to better understand the artist's *magnum opus* by exploring its broader historical context: a time when science-fiction manga was experiencing a rebirth, many years after Osamu Tezuka's *Tetsuwan Atomu* (*Astro Boy*) and Mitsuteru Yokoyama's *Tetsujin 28-go*, the latter serving as an inspiration for *Akira*.

We will primarily explore *Akira* through the socio-historical echo of its many themes: the memory of the Pacific Wars, the trauma of Hiroshima and Nagasaki, the student revolts of the late sixties, the worrisome speed of local economic progress, the culture of the so-called *bosozoku* bikers, the necessary and logical emergence of cyberpunk in Japan, etc. Such an approach is essential if we are to fully understand the "Japaneseness" of Katsuhiro Otomo's manga.

So, let's revisit the impact of *Akira*, the manga series that turned everything on its head.

About the Author:

Rémi Lopez holds a B.A. in Japanese culture and civilization. His interest in RPGs dates back to childhood. This passion has endured: at age seventeen, he wrote his very first articles for the specialized magazines *Gameplay RPG* and *Role Playing Game*, after having made his debut on the Internet as a gaming enthusiast. A great admirer of Jung, Campbell, and Eliade, he launched his career as an author, writing two *Final Fantasy* books published by Third Éditions. The first, in 2013, dealt with the franchise's eighth episode while the second, in 2015, explored the universe of Ivalice. He has since coauthored two more works devoted to the *Persona* saga. Rémi Lopez has also written *Cowboy Bebop: Deep Space Blues* and *The Legend of Chrono Trigger*, also published by Third Éditions.

THE IMPACT OF AKIRA

A MANGA [R]EVOLUTION

1.1: Creation: Conception

"When my publishers approached me about having my work translated for publication abroad, I was admittedly skeptical. Akira was created for Japanese readers in a Japanese context. I wondered what a Western or American audience could possibly get out of it. Obviously, I was wrong. [...] I wrote the story a long time ago, but hindsight allows me to look at it more objectively. It's an anti-establishment work. The fact that other artists continue to draw inspiration from Akira undoubtedly means that the work remains relevant today."

Katsuhiro Otomo, 2016[1]

Thirty-seven years after its first chapter was published, *Akira* still provokes. In the world of pop culture, Katsuhiro Otomo's influence is undeniable. A tribute to subversion, *Akira*'s themes and cyberpunk atmosphere seem to increasingly embody today's world. The present and future are closing in on one another, almost to the point of merging: aren't the 2020 Olympic Games scheduled to take place in Tokyo, like in Otomo's manga series? Mightn't we see clandestine motorcycle races and monster demonstrations repressed by the police?

Akira is a mixture of both the universal and the specifically Japanese, a rich cocktail of varied influences reflecting the career of its genius author. Curious by nature, Otomo has an insatiable interest in other cultures, although his body of work prior to *Akira* still remains relatively unknown outside of Japan. And yet within Japan, Otomo was regarded as one of the truly great manga artists well before *Akira*'s publication. He spearheaded a new generation that would push back the boundaries of their creative medium. Otomo is not a troublemaker: he is a dissident. Everything he does, he does of his own accord. At a time when publishers had not yet appropriated all of the industry's decision-making powers, he made his own choices, never worrying about the opinions of others. The artist thus permitted himself a great deal of freedom during his formative years. Before the immense success of *Akira*, he boldly experimented with various

1. Stéphane Jarno, "Katsuhiro Otomo: *Akira* is an anti-establishment work," *Télérama*, June 17, 2016.

registers, from the noir to the absurd and from the tender to the distasteful. No one could say that his work had been rehashed. According to Otomo, his curiosity stems from a personal desire: "Most people probably want to express everything that they have inside, but guys like me want to do something totally new every time. Maybe it's more important to value your own ideas." And Otomo sowed his ideas in dozens of short stories for almost a decade before embarking on what would become his most celebrated work: *Akira*. Otomo's influence on both science fiction and the cyberpunk movement–which, in the early 1980s, needed pillars on which to build itself–was significant. But even more importantly, the work of the man who created *Akira* was decisive for an entire generation of manga artists. He was the silent figurehead of the manga revival, an idea that is supported by Hisashi Eguchi, one of Otomo's collaborators: "Back then, there were only a few manga artists being hailed as part of this movement called the New Wave. But, as far as I was concerned, Otomo was the only true New Wave artist."

Katsuhiro Otomo was born on April 14, 1954 in the former city of Hasama, now part of Tome, in the Miyagi Prefecture. Since it was essentially a rural area, Otomo spent a good deal of his childhood binging on manga. He read the great classics, which included *Tetsuwan Atomu* (*Astro Boy*) written by Osamu Tezuka–often referred to as "the god of manga"– as well as Mitsuteru Yokoyama's *Tetsujin 28-go* and Jiro Kuwata's *8 Man*: *shonen* manga that soon became legendary as each release was devoured by Otomo's generation. But for Otomo, reading was essentially a solitary activity. As the only boy among both younger and older sisters, he was regularly given manga that he read in seclusion, sometimes copying his idols' illustrations, before being able to buy it on his own (but no more than one per month, that was the rule). He also had the opportunity to witness the emergence of the very first Japanese animated feature films at a very young age: thirty years before his adaptation of *Akira* made audiences shiver in darkened theaters, Taiji Yabushita's *Hakujaden* (*Panda and the Magic Serpent*, 1958) and Tezuka's *Saiyuki* (*Alakazam the Great*, 1960) filled his young mind with wonder. When his favorite series were adapted into weekly anime broadcasts for the masses, Otomo's passion took on a new dimension. No longer did he have to go to the cinema to see motion pictures, he could watch his heroes' adventures at home on TV.

Otomo's reading preferences evolved along with those of his generation. As the core audience targeted by Tezuka and other artists grew older, the market naturally evolved, creating a demand for teenage, and even adult, manga. And while Otomo's interest in *shonen* did not entirely wane, his entry into adolescence triggered the need for more explosive content. This came in the form of *gekiga*, which literally translates into "dramatic pictures." Rather than being considered a subgenre of manga (i.e. "humorous pictures"), *gekiga* is generally considered a genre in its own right. Although the two are similar, *gekiga* is more realistic and less "cartoonish." Unapologetic in its display of brute force and violence, it is characterized by much darker graphics. We owe the term *gekiga* to one of its greatest artists, Yoshihiro Tatsumi. He baptized the new genre as early as 1957, after parents were outraged by the presence of such illustrations next to innocent children's issues. The ensuing confusion subsequently lead to the labeling of these adult manga series.[2] Created in 1964 by Sanpei Shirato (*Sasuke*, the *Kamui* Series), *Garo*[3] was the flagship magazine for this new genre. It featured various artists: not only Tatsumi, but also the enigmatic Yoshiharu Tsuge and the brilliant Shigeru Mizuki (*GeGeGe no Kitaro* aka *Kitaro of the Graveyard*), whose meticulous designs were particularly appreciated by Otomo. Even Osamu Tezuka, a shrewd entrepreneur as well as a great artist, jumped on the *gekiga* bandwagon by publishing *COM*, his very own magazine dedicated to avant-garde manga, in 1967. It was in these very pages that the young Otomo discovered a new type of manga. This discovery enabled him to envision the possibility of using manga to say something, to get various messages across and paint a vitriolic picture of the world's harshness. Later, he explained that the change was inevitable: "When my generation started making manga in the 1970s, we were reading *Ashita no Joe* and *Kyojin no Hoshi*, and the stories just kept getting darker. Even in other genres, it was a strange time: film had its own New Wave, while drama had Shuji Terayama and the Black Tent Troupe. In the midst of all that, it was a foregone conclusion that manga would also become dark and moody." Beyond its subject matter, *gekiga*'s gloomy atmosphere came from its settings and their great narrative value. If the plot revolved around a hard-boiled detective, for example, the dirty, poorly-lit nighttime neighborhoods and rain set the tone. There is no doubt that Otomo's work was significantly influenced by *gekiga* and the emphasis it placed on atmosphere. Very early on, he endeavored to turn his settings into characters in their own right.

Otomo had not yet taken any drawing lessons, and the future manga artist's scribbles lacked genuine professionalism. It wasn't until he discovered Shotaro Ishinomori's didactic book *Mangaka Nyumon* (which can be roughly translated as *Introduction to Becoming a Manga Artist*) that Otomo, then a

2. Jean-Marie Bouissou. *Manga – Histoire et Univers de la Bande Dessinée Japonaise*. Picquier Poche, 2013.
3. Despite its status as a cult magazine, it never sold more than 80,000 copies per issue.

schoolboy, began to take his passion more seriously. This work, published in 1965, became a bible for the budding artist, as it did for many young illustrators of his age. Otomo was indeed a big fan of Ishinomori (*Cyborg 009*, *Sarutobi Ecchan* aka *Hela Supergirl*), whose high school he even attended! As his ambition grew, Otomo assiduously followed Ishinomori's instructions and honed his craft. Only then did he take the plunge and begin illustrating his own stories. At age fifteen, he participated in a talent contest organized by *Shonen Sunday* magazine. He submitted five pages of a work entitled *Sogeki*. Similar to Takao Saito's *Golgo 13*, it was the tale of an assassin for hire, and he received an honorable mention. Otomo's attempts before age nineteen were failures despite regular professional encouragement; *COM* magazine even published a page of his *Umi ga...* in its February 1971 issue. In December of the same year, he penned what can be considered his first major "work," an adaptation of Andersen's *The Little Match Girl*, which took up over sixty pages, two of which were unearthed by the magazine *Pafu* in 1979, in an issue celebrating the artist's career.

Otomo's entry into high school was synonymous with important changes in the young man's life, as his growing interest in cinema gradually pushed him down new artistic paths. During these years, Otomo went to as many feature films as possible. No matter how long the train ride to Sendai took, he was adamant about seeing his favorite directors' works. Despite his young age, he had a penchant for directors who were beloved by film buffs but not necessarily known for their accessibility. Among these were Luis Buñuel, who made the controversial film *Un Chien Andalou* (aka *An Andalusian Dog* - 1929), Frank Capra, the great Ingmar Bergman, Sergei Eisenstein, and French film director Julien Duvivier. Otomo soon became interested in bold, experimental cinema—he still enjoys watching Federico Fellini's films when he is overwhelmed by fatigue—but this did not prevent him from appreciating the classic works of Akira Kurosawa, Yasujiro Ozu, and Japanese cinema in general. He particularly enjoys provocative, avant-garde movies, especially those of Shohei Imamura, whose praises he has always sung.[4] And it is this seductively subversive quality, this art of overturning codes, that he ultimately appreciated in the cinematic movement that truly influenced him: that of New Hollywood.

The New Hollywood movement was spearheaded by a counterculture that could taste its own freedom. Its passionate and ambitious directors were determined to redefine cinema, while pushing its boundaries, both in terms of its substance and its mode of production. Beginning in the mid-1960s, an entire generation of young directors came to prominence in the United

---

4. Whether it was a tribute or just a coincidence, Otomo named his son (born in 1980) Shohei.

States. They did not recognize themselves in the tired Hollywood machine of their era, which was lacking not only in inspiration but also success. Otomo's free spirit was echoed in the aimless journeys of Peter Fonda and Dennis Hopper in *Easy Rider* (Dennis Hopper, 1969), in the suicidal and tragic duo of Warren Beatty and Faye Dunaway in the legendary *Bonnie and Clyde* (Arthur Penn, 1967) and, above all, in the hymn to peace and independence that was Michael Wadleigh's *Woodstock* documentary (1970), whose three-hour run time[5] immersed viewers in the human warmth of the world's most famous rock festival. The young Otomo no longer thought of films or manga in the same way. Life itself, by his own admission, had taken on new meaning. Otomo discovered a certain pleasure in seeing characters with glaring weaknesses, magnificent anti-heroes waging losing battles, an echo, perhaps, of the student revolts that were taking place all over the world at that time, and especially in Japan (a movement that failed after the renewal of the Japan-US Security Treaty in 1970, as we will later see). Sam Peckinpah's *Straw Dogs* (1971), which admittedly isn't to everyone's taste, also left a profound mark on Otomo due to its crescendo of raw, unspeakable violence, not to mention the unveiling of its protagonists' true nature. All of these films also revolved around the longing to "pack up and leave town," a desire that the future manga artist had shared for quite some time.

And despite cinema's increasing pull, Otomo continued to draw. His style began to evolve as new influences took hold: "When I was younger, I tried to draw very traditional manga-like art. I tried to imitate *Astro Boy* and stuff like that. But, when I was in high school, the illustrations of people like Yokoo Tadanori and Isaka Yoshitaro became quite popular, and I ended up really appreciating their artistic styles. I decided that I wanted to adopt it for my own manga. I wanted to create characters using this type of approach, rather than sticking to the classic style. I wanted my manga to have more of an illustration feel to it, I suppose."

Otomo was planning on moving to Tokyo despite his parents' warnings that he was too young to leave home. What would he do for money? Why give up on going to art school? According to Otomo, he found that route dismally academic. And anyway, moving to Tokyo at age nineteen, well that was something every manga artist did! Otomo was looking for something more honest, a rawer form of expression than the one promised by classical channels: meeting the authors at *COM* was one of his goals. At the time, many of his contemporaries were eking out a living by creating *seishun*

---

5. This run time refers to the original film that came out in 1970. The longer (1994) version is over four hours long.

manga, slices of life about ordinary young people, often forced to work hard to meet ends meet. The sincerity of this type of manga appealed to a certain type of audience. During his high school years, Otomo had met an editor from Futabasha through a mutual friend (the manga artist Moribi Murano). The editor in question worked for the magazine *Manga Action*, created in 1967 and considered the first real *seinen* magazine (featuring works like *Lupin III* by Monkey Punch and *Lone Wolf and Cub* by Kazuo Koike and Goseki Kojima). Surprised by the quality of Otomo's drawings, the editor, who was based in Tokyo, suggested that they get in touch once the young man graduated from high school. This proposal did not fall on deaf ears. Otomo was recruited after just one phone call.

Following a visit to Nippori, where he succeeded in securing lodging with friends, Otomo moved to the Saitama Prefecture, in what was then the small town of Minami-Urawa, a stone's throw from Tokyo, where many of the town's inhabitants went to work early in the morning. According to Otomo, "Minami-Urawa was fascinating. There were lots of little bars nearby, and bars in a place like Minami-Urawa, Saitama tend to be run by and for folks from the regions. So there were people who looked like *yakuza*, the odd pervy-looking gangster type ... a really intriguing bunch. I was only there for four years, but it was quite an education, I can tell you." Otomo's careful observation of the people around him served as one of his major sources of inspiration. Rather than prolonged encounters, it was the little things, the details, that were important to the artist: "Although there's a point in time when I create stories in my head, my initial ideas come to me when I go out to people-watch, at a bookstore, a CD shop, a bar, and so forth. [...] In my early twenties I often took the train to catch a movie. But I almost enjoyed observing the person seated opposite me on the train more than I did watching the film. 'His shoes are worn out, so maybe he's a traveling salesman' or 'he's a bit pale, so he's probably really tired'—carrying on this vein, I could imagine anyone's work life. And watching children in the park, perhaps I'd think: 'it's kids' clumsiness that makes them so cute.' This is how a story emerges, how a manga series develops. I think it's the same for musicians who really 'connect' with their music."

In August 1973, Katsuhiro Otomo finally saw his first story, *Jusei* aka *Gun Report*, published in *Manga Action* (he also created the cover of this issue). The story, however, wasn't an original: it was a rather loose adaptation of *Mateo Falcone*, a novella by the French writer Prosper Mérimée (subtitled *The Ways of Corsica*) published in 1829. Otomo was barely nineteen years old at the time and, although his style still lacked character, one could already see his penchant for detail (especially in his settings) not to mention a very cinematographic audacity in terms of both viewing angles and framing. Because the young artist attached great importance to both illustration and film, his manga had to appropriate their domain-specific languages to fit his images. Otomo published four other stories that same year. Among these were *Shinyu*, based on Edgar Allen Poe's short story *William Wilson*, and *Sumairii Ojisan*, an adaptation of Mark Twain's *The Celebrated Jumping Frog of Calaveras County*.

It wasn't uncommon for the manga artists of Otomo's generation—and generations prior—to look to European and American fiction. The beginning of the twentieth century saw the development of *kyoyo-shugi* in Japan, a movement that established culture (*kyoyo*), which included prestigious Western literature, as a fundamental instrument of healthy (and yes, elite) personal development. The first manga artists were the heirs of this philosophy, as Eiji Oguma has pointed out: "Outstanding manga artists referenced *kyoyo-shugi* in their memoirs. People like Fujio Akatsuka, Shotaro Ishinomori, and Fujiko Fujio recounted their extensive exposure to European and American films and literature while residing in the Tokiwa-So apartment house (famous for the number of young manga artists who lived there in the 1950s). According to an interview with Akatsuka, when they visited the famous manga artist Osamu Tezuka, the latter told them, 'If you want to become great manga artists, don't read manga. It's more important that you watch first-rate films, listen to first-rate music, read first-rate books, and see first-rate theater performances.' Akatsuka often adapted short stories by Charles Dickens and the like, while Ishinomori's tales were inspired by European and American science fiction and panels dedicated to the adaptation of European films."[6]

Otomo's early career essentially consisted of short publications, sufficiently spaced out in time so as to avoid high expectations. Given his young age and audacity, the artist's talent was indeed promising, but nothing seemed to point to the success he would ultimately enjoy. Many thought that his artwork's realistic sobriety and lack of pizazz would condemn him to oblivion, a fate shared by numerous manga artists. During a conference held in 2008, Kentaro Takekuma explained that these traits were not shortcomings originating from a lack of inspiration, but rather deliberate choices intended to give a certain "crispness" to Otomo's work: "We can view these early Otomo sketches, with their subdued art and scripts, as the antithesis to *gekiga*, which was at the height of its popularity during

6. Eiji Oguma. "An Industry Awaiting Reform: The Social Origins and Economics of Manga and Animation in Postwar Japan." *The Asia-Pacific Journal*, vol. 15, issue 9, no. 1, April 2017.

this time. [...] [Otomo's manga] followed the realistic art tradition that the *gekiga* movement started, while boldly rejecting the expressionistic techniques that it developed (panel frames extending beyond the page, super-dense motion lines, standardized poses during action scenes, and so on)." This idea echoes Otomo's perspective in a 1988 interview, when he'd gained enough hindsight to better understand his career: "At the time, neither I nor any of my companions had our eyes set on the big magazines. Truth be told, we didn't even aspire to create particularly interesting or amusing works (laughs). We weren't overly concerned with plots, endings, or the like. We were quite enthusiastic about the idea of using manga to show how we lived and what we were thinking. I guess in those days, we saw manga as a genre akin to literature. Drawing manga is about expressing oneself, so back then artists and their work were highly idiosyncratic. That was when the manga world was at its most robust." Another aspect of Otomo's art that tended to distinguish him from others—and perhaps one of the most easily recognizable—was his preference for fine-nibbed pens. *Gekiga* artists frequently used the G-pen, a thick-nibbed pen that enabled them to draw exaggerated features and flesh out their characters. This was partly what gave the genre its dark and occasionally grimy look. A much finer nibbed-pen, the maru-pen, was then used to sharpen the details, as well as the background and setting. Otomo used the maru-pen for absolutely everything, and he was criticized for doing so. Many people thought his drawings were too "flat" and that his characters failed to stand out. But that was precisely the point: to make the hero a full-fledged actor, thus integrating both man and plot.

Otomo's manga also demonstrated his indifference to climactic endings. As in *Easy Rider*, narratives don't necessarily conclude with the resolution of a problem—assuming there is one! Instead, they often end abruptly, with no accountability to the reader/viewer. In this respect, they imitate life. And although *gekiga* was at the height of its popularity, Otomo didn't want to succumb to the idea of noir for noir's sake, i.e. the use of graphic violence as a mere tool to "shock." The violence in Otomo's manga was more subtle, because it was more honest. He eschewed unnecessary artifice. In April 1974, Otomo penned *Boogie Woogie Waltz*, his oldest story to have been included in a compilation (first in *Good Weather*, published in 1981, and then in its spiritual sequel—a compilation of the same name—the following year). Over the span of twenty-three pages, the manga relates the senti-mental, sexual, and more generally existential wanderings of a young man working in a clothing shop, who falls in love with a prostitute and tries to rein in his death drives. Otomo made no attempt to turn his protagonist into an antihero: the young man in question simply endures his life, in an urban jungle, with no relief in sight. The narrative's solidity is of little importance here. Instead, it is the tale's flexibility that allows Otomo to portray a raw reality, one that is both trivial and yet often touching. *Suka to Sukkiri* aka *Refreshment*, published in August 1975, features the same type of "loser" who, unable to stand the oppressive heat of Tokyo, attempts to steal a fan, but fails miserably. He then tries to pilfer someone else's, but the household he chooses doesn't have one, so he subsequently ties up the inhabitants and then helps himself to the family's... refrigerator! Otomo's dark humor tends to shine through in aimless stories like these. Many of his tales combine both misery and ineptitude, saying much more about the human condition than tales with a "classic" structure. This seemingly sterile type of plot was a direct reflection of Otomo's experience in the bars of Minami-Urawa. His characters' appearance is much more telling than any lengthy dialogue could be: "After my experiences in those bars, I never looked at anyone in a superficial way again. As I observed people, both rich and poor, I started to think that everyone was trying their hardest, dealing with all sorts of terrible things. I was drawn to individuals like that, decided I liked people and all of their foibles. Once I started thinking this way, stories that fit into conventional patterns became too boring. I wanted to try drawing real people, people beyond the limits of anything I could possibly imagine."

Shusei Sanchi no Yukie-san (July 1976) is one of the artist's more disturbing stories, proving that, despite his young age, he didn't consider any subject taboo. We see very young children—fascinated by what they are watching on TV—exploring their anatomy without really understanding the significance of their actions. *Okasu*, which appeared the following month, dealt with rape, and the line between dark humor and the truly sinister was even more blurred. In this twenty-five-page tale (this was typically the length of Otomo's manga), a small, puny worker decides to rape a high school girl, but she ultimately gains the upper hand and beats him up. Otomo was only in his early twenties when he began addressing explosive themes, but we should remember that the manga artist was also being influenced by equally subversive directors, such as Sam Peckinpah, who depicted the rape of his hero's wife in *Straw Dogs* for several long minutes: a scene that caused a great deal of controversy when it came out, especially because the victim ended up enjoying herself.

Otomo's productivity was increasing year after year: a sign that *Manga Action* had growing confidence in him and that there was an audience for his work. The manga artist's brutally realistic, and sometimes wacky, slices of life continued to grow in popularity, as is evidenced by *Uchu Patrol Sigma* aka *Space Patrolman Shigema*, published in February 1977. In this work, friends—who are spending an evening drinking together—each reveal that they come from different planets, the last one confessing that he is a "space sheriff" whose laser gun resembles a penis. Three months later, Otomo penned *Nothing Will Be As It Was*, which once again combined the absurd and the sordid. In it, he portrayed a young man's panic while trying to dispose of the body of his friend, whom he has just killed (with a hammer) in his apartment. Nothing is spared, from the bleeding of the corpse to its dismemberment, and the protagonist finally decides to store the body parts in his refrigerator for future consumption. Like much of Otomo's manga, the story never becomes too serious, but what is most impressive is his mastery of rhythm. The first pages linger on the quivering protagonist's panic, his awkwardness, and the lost, ultimately desperate look in his eyes. Several panels have no text, and Otomo even cuts to a succession of gestures leading to the lighting of a cigarette, before the murderer deigns to open his mouth (and we begin to understand what may have motivated his act). The narrative has no conclusion as such: we simply see the murderer resign himself to sticking his victim's body parts in the refrigerator. There's no investigation or further follow-up.

The year 1977 marked an important turning point in Otomo's career, as this was the year he first tackled a relatively lengthy story. The five installments of *Sayonara Nippon* were published in *Manga Action* (between August 1977 and February 1978) and relate the misadventures of a penniless young Japanese karate practitioner trying to earn a living in New York City by teaching his discipline (a story that was probably inspired, at least in part, by Otomo's honeymoon in New York—incidentally, he also profited from his honeymoon to attend a Bob Marley concert). Culture shock then hits our protagonist, both hard and literally, when a former (six-and-a-half-foot-tall) boxer challenges—and easily pulverizes—him, and again, when he defends a young woman without realizing that he's taking on a gang... The young karate practitioner's candor makes him the ultimate loser, a clueless good guy who, like so many others, is just trying to get by with his limited understanding of life. *Sayonara Nippon* also embodies a certain aspect of Otomo's art, one that many recognized as revolutionary at the time. In it, he highlighted the ethnicity of his characters, especially the Japanese, something that was extremely rare in the 1970s. *Okasu*'s title page, which shows a close-up of his young heroine's face, is particularly telling. She has slanted eyes and a low nose, far from the manga standards of the time. Seen from a distance, you could mistake the drawing for a photograph. Nevertheless, Otomo wasn't going for absolute realism in his subject matter (or even his characters' appearance): "I've always paid attention to two key aspects: fantasy and realism. If you neglect one for the other, it weakens the story. Depicting things too realistically actually damages the work's social realism, while delving too far into the realm of fantasy sabotages the imaginative aspect. I'm always thinking about how to balance the two. I think the realism of my early works stems from the fact that I used close friends as character models. My style naturally relies on observation."

In 1978, Otomo also began to work on a series of (loose) adaptations of children's stories and other literary classics, which were compiled in the volume *Hansel and Gretel* (published in 1981). The artist's work thus began to appear in more and more magazines, including *Young Action, Rocking'On, Pop Corn,* and even *Vampirella.* Otomo explained this fragmented dissemination in 1979: "*Hansel and Gretel* was a long time in the making. I worked on it between jobs, without a clue as to where I'd publish it. No one at *(Manga) Action* was interested in hearing about *Hansel and Gretel.* Nor did anyone comment much when I showed it to them. [...] *Hansel and Gretel* was entirely the result of my own personal desire to draw." Inspired by the Dutch painter Bruegel's creatures and backgrounds, Otomo thus created one of his lesser-known works on the sly, a work that is still of considerable artistic value today.[7] The impressive precision of each drawing confirmed Otomo's love of details, which was about to be recognized by a wider public thanks to his future successes. And among these successes was *Fireball.*

In early 1979, Otomo penned his very first science fiction work, *Fireball,*[8] published in *Action Deluxe* magazine. He explained that this change of register was, once again, a personal choice: "I have guilty memories of telling [my editors] that I only wanted to do sci-fi. This was the era of children's comics, ones like *Dousei Jidai* and *Jukyoden,* and I wanted to do something different. I persuaded my editor to let me write a hardcore sci-fi story, and this title was the result. [...] Until then, I'd been depicting real everyday people, and I started to feel like my narratives were becoming too similar. I guess I just got tired of what I was doing. I wasn't looking to develop a particular style. I just wanted to keep on doing new things, avoid falling into a rut." At the time, the sci-fi genre was booming, both in the West with the *Star Wars* phenomenon, and in Japan with the revival brought on by *Space Battleship Yamato, Galaxy Express 999,* and *Mobile Suit Gundam.* Otomo has even admitted to being influenced by *Star Wars.* Could it have been the telekinetic powers of the Force that appealed to him? *Fireball* is about fifty pages long. Although the story remains unfinished and fizzles out a bit at the end, the influence of this first attempt was

7. Otomo paid homage to Bruegel and his famous painting *The Tower of Babel* not once, but twice: first in 1984, when he penned a Canon brand advertisement showing the tower in a more futuristic context, and again in 2017, when he created *Inside Babel,* a magnificent cutaway painting depicting his vision of the tower's interior.
8. The title is a reference to a song by Deep Purple, following the example of Otomo's *Highway Star* compilation released the same year.

unparalleled both with respect to the public and Otomo himself. One could already see the beginnings of *Akira* in *Fireball*, so close are their codes and themes.

Fireball takes place in a megalopolis shaken by massive anti-government demonstrations. Those in power are secretly working on the development of a supercomputer called ATOM (a reference to Osamu Tezuka's *Astro Boy*, known in Japan by its original name *Mighty Atom*), which should eventually give them absolute control of the city. The story follows two brothers, on opposite sides: the younger brother is a revolutionary who has found out about ATOM and seeks to destroy it, while the older brother is a member of the police force. Both have developed their telekinetic powers since childhood, especially the older one, whose skills are of interest to the computer. Under the guise of a medical examination, the older brother is anesthetized and subsequently dismembered. And, although this is never entirely made clear, this is because ATOM is looking to turn his body into a flesh and blood host. Things go from bad to worse when the police shoot the younger brother, riddling him with bullets. This causes the older brother's sleeping consciousness (still on the operating table) to react. Having reached a higher level of consciousness, he regains control of his body, which is still in pieces, and generates heat waves powerful enough to destroy everything around him for miles, before going to confront the ATOM central unit. The last image shows the two brothers, the younger one having been "resurrected" by the resonance of their brain waves, floating above the exploding government installations.

Years later, in his first anthology, Otomo clarified what he had intended to do with *Fireball*: "Originally, it was supposed to be a much simpler story about a group of freedom fighters out to destroy the Director's evil computer, but it morphed into a tale about psychic superpowers. I didn't come up with the name *Fireball* until after the work was finished. The ending was going to be a battle between the heat of the psychic superhuman and the cold of the computer whilst the temperature rose around them, and then the computer would end up analyzing the secret of the psychic's power and turn it against him, whereupon the younger brother, who claimed he didn't have the power, would manifest it after all. That's the original script I wrote, but it was too obscure. So, I decided to redraw the scene, with the characters combining their powers to overcome the computer, and the last scene is one in which the two heroes, looking down on the Earth from outer space, talk over old times."

A society on the verge of implosion, an all-powerful government, a mad experiment that turns against its creators, and telekinetic powers: all of *Fireball*'s premises could just as easily be used to describe *Akira*. And, in terms of graphics, Otomo continued to innovate. His maps of the besieged city are extremely rich, while his frames portraying the elder brother's dismembered body, rising from the operating table, marked an entire generation of readers, who immediately became Otomo fans. Among them was a prominent representative of the next generation, Naoki Urasawa, who enjoyed a huge success with his masterpiece *Monster* (1994-2001) as well as the no less excellent *20th Century Boys* (1999-2006). Urasawa, who has always had a great deal of praise for Otomo, recalled the moment he discovered *Fireball*: "*Fireball* just goes on plunking down scene after scene without narration. It was different from the conventional rhythm in Japanese manga and more like something lifted from Kubrick or Peckinpah—the stuff that we considered hip, right there in a manga. [...] And because of *Fireball*, everyone draws this way now, and I mean absolutely everyone, myself included. Part of manga is about pulling things off with the bare minimum of lines, about how a well-placed line changes the way things look. When I met Otomo, I told him that for us, *Fireball* was our *New Treasure Island* [Tezuka's first major work]. Just as Fujiko Fujio and Shotaro Ishinomori were blown away by that opening scene with the car in Osamu Tezuka's *New Treasure Island*, we were blown away by *Fireball*. It opened the door. It was the beginning of the manga of our age." It was a new era that would erase the codes of the previous one from which it was inspired. It has even been reported that Tezuka, upon seeing Otomo's rich and detailed drawings, exclaimed: "If that's manga, I don't want to make it!"

And although Otomo never finished *Fireball*, having "grown bored" after about twenty pages, his change in register (embodied by his move toward science fiction) would continue in subsequent years, in both short and long stories, not to mention the massive work *Akira*. Without abandoning his slice of life portrayals, which often revolved around music—as in *So What?* (June 1978), *East of the Sun, West of the Moon* (March 1979), and *Seijiga Machini Yattekiru* (May 1979), where the ethnicity of characters was once again emphasized—Otomo tried his hand at experimental science fiction. Such works include the very short *Flower* (October 1979), a silent and colorful story in which a soldier waters a plant in the middle of an apocalyptic landscape before being crushed by a biomechanical creature, who goes on to use the unfortunate man's blood to water the plant himself, and the equally short *Sound of Sand* (November 1979), in which an astronaut sinks into the quicksand of a desert planet before being rescued by his comrades, who discover that there is nothing left in their colleague's suit but sand... which then starts to move and attack them!

9. Naoto Yamakawa adapted this story for the cinema in 1988.

It was around this time that Otomo was introduced to the work of an artist who would greatly influence him: the Frenchman Jean Giraud, aka Mœbius. Otomo's use of color in *Flower* was a direct consequence of this encounter. Otomo spoke of his reaction upon seeing the artist's work: "I had rarely felt such emotion. His style, his sketches, and the intensely personal universe he created: it was new. At the time, manga was based on shadow play. Simple Moebius-like features were reserved for children's books. Little by little, I bought all of his graphic novels. I especially liked *The Incal.* Unfortunately, only the very first volumes of his work had been translated into Japanese. Later, I supervised the Japanese translation of some of his books, and we met several times. He was definitely a product of the seventies. A real hippie. At one point, we were working on a project to adapt *The Airtight Garage* for the cinema. *Arzach* is still my favorite collection. I guess I wasn't the only one who was impressed by it. Jiro Taniguchi, Akira Toriyama, and a number of other Japanese illustrators owe a great deal to Moebius." Otomo and the French artist became quite good friends, a bond that was symbolized by Moebius' gift to Otomo: a pen made from the branch of a tree in his garden!

The late seventies and early eighties were undoubtedly the most prosperous and productive period of Otomo's career, before all his time was taken up by his magnum opus, *Akira.* By the end of the seventies, new readers could discover his already rich body of work, with the release of *tankobon*[10] compiling some of his manga: *Short Peace* and *Highway Star* in 1979, then *Good Weather, Sayonara Nippon,* and *Hansel and Gretel* in 1981. To attest to this growing success, the monthly magazine *Pafu* even devoted its July 1979 issue to Otomo, looking back over his already impressive career while discussing his influences... and his cat!

Then came the 1980s. The decade that was to propel Otomo to the rank of manga superstar began with fanfare, with *Action Deluxe*'s publication of *Domu,* the work that is now considered a prequel to his masterpiece, *Akira.* (*Domu* was subtitled *A Child's Dream* in the publication by Dark Horse Comics.) *Action Deluxe* had only accorded him about fifty pages, which Otomo thought would be enough at first. However, it didn't take long for the manga artist to realize that he had embarked on something much larger, as was the case with *Fireball. Domu* takes place in a neighborhood similar to Otomo's own at the time, an impersonal concrete monster that the artist came to appreciate in his own way: "A huge new public housing complex was built while I was living in the area. It was soon filled with

---

10. Bound compilations, typically including several chapters of a manga previously published in the magazines.

low-income couples and their newborn babies. They never seemed to adapt to the crowded urban living conditions, and I think they felt trapped in that environment. Nonetheless, I enjoyed being around those people." In terms of work, all he needed was a little inspiration to get started: "I had a sense of [*Domu*'s] basic plot, but I couldn't decide where to set the story. I was reading a newspaper one day, and a brief article caught my eye. It reported that dozens of people living in the Takashima-Daira Estates (a huge public housing complex on the outskirts of Tokyo) committed suicide every year. They jumped off the buildings. I suddenly realized that I'd found the setting for *Domu*." There were probably tons of stories behind those concrete walls—and their uniform rows of tiny balconies—and Otomo liked to imagine them in minute detail. The manga artist associated the deadly Takashima-Daira Estates with a short story he had recently read: a narrative, by Algernon Blackwood, in which two powerful characters prepare to do silent battle. He also wanted to give his new work a horrific atmosphere, a desire motivated by William Friedkin's film *The Exorcist* (1973), which he had seen while working on *Fireball*. And, while Otomo never specifically mentioned David Cronenberg's film *Scanners* (1981), the purely psychic fight between his two adversaries bore a strong resemblance to those of the movie.

Domu differed from Otomo's previous works due to the simple fact that it was a carefully built, structured story with a "true ending." As the artist himself has stated, he wanted his manga to have a film-like quality, with his readers feeling as if they had just left the movie theater: "With *Domu* I thought carefully about the composition: how I could pull the reader along and hold their interest." *Domu* is a mix of horror and science fiction. It is set against the backdrop of a police investigation in a neighborhood where more and more strange deaths are occurring. While the police are floundering, following false leads, the reader quickly discovers the truth: the deaths that have engendered constant paranoia amongst the neighborhood inhabitants are in reality murders, perpetrated by the last person anyone suspects, a senile old man by the name of Chojiro Uchida, known as "old Cho." He possesses supernatural abilities that the police can't even begin to fathom. And it's not the police who will eventually save the day, but Etsuko (aka Ecchan[11]), a little girl who has powers similar to old Cho's. Unlike the adults, she isn't at all fooled by the old man. Their duel takes on surrealist proportions, resulting in a titanic battle in the second half of the story. It destroys much of the neighborhood, giving one an idea of how *Fireball* might have ended and prefiguring the ruinous landscapes of *Akira*.

11. A reference to *Sarutobi Ecchan*, a manga series by Shotaro Ishinomori.

While the existence of supernatural elements in a very ordinary neighborhood (dehumanized by agonizingly uniform architecture and inhabited by people with no real history) was fascinating, it was Otomo's graphic work that really left a lasting impression. *Domu*'s brilliance stems from Otomo's painstaking attention to detail, especially in terms of setting. He took the time to draw several neighborhood buildings in their entirety, as evidenced in the very first frames. This is particularly apparent in chapter 5, when there is a huge explosion in the far end of one building, and Otomo is careful to include even the smallest of details. Otomo's tendency to "give it his all" transforms the setting into a prominent feature, an omnipresent, unavoidable concrete monster whose impersonal aspect takes on terrifying proportions, much like the corridors of the Overlook Hotel in Kubrick's *The Shining* (1980) or the sinister building in Hideo Nakata's *Dark Water* (2002). Such terror takes on a new dimension as the duel between Etsuko and old Cho turns into a destructive chase, with the two opponents manipulating gravity. Otomo thus changes up his viewing angles and blurs the landmarks: tops and bottoms merge until the buildings' facades resemble the evolving faces of a Chinese puzzle, leaving the viewer feeling both lost and disoriented. According to the artist, it's only possible to exploit this gigantism in comics and manga: "Unlike animation, you can use extremely wide compositions and biframes. So, if you really want someone to spend time looking at a picture, you can draw it big. You can't do that with animation. It's a huge limitation. Every scene is drawn in the same proportion and size." Otomo's perspectives systematically highlight the setting, as is this case when Etsuko is shown sitting on a swing. The drawing spreads out above her, revealing almost the entire building—sad and inert—as it looms in the background. The scale is absolutely terrifying.

At any rate, *Domu*'s release remained rather chaotic. Of its six chapters, only the first four were published in magazines: chapters one through three appeared in *Action Deluxe*, then after the latter was discontinued, the fourth was published in *Manga Action Super Fiction*. It took two years for the remainder of the story to be published in a final *tankobon* that came out in 1983, affording Otomo enough time to fine-tune his work. This delay in publication didn't affect its success with the Japanese public: 500,000 people bought copies so that they could see how the story ended, with the growing success of *Akira* undoubtedly playing a role. Public and critical acclaim also contributed, as *Domu* won the Nihon SF Taisho Grand Prize in 1983, a first for a manga, which caused a bit of controversy. Those who were most bitter cited the scarcity of science fiction that year, a view that was denounced by the famous author Sakyo Komatsu (who had enjoyed great success with his disaster novel *Japan Sinks* ten years earlier). He declared that Otomo's work was entirely worthy of the prize. Here again,

Naoki Urasawa recalled his shock upon reading the story: "When the first episode of *Domu* came out, I saw the cover with a polar bear on it [the January 1980 issue of *Action Deluxe*]. I wondered what it was, and a little later I learned that there was an Otomo manga in that issue. I ran to the bookstore. There was only one copy left, and it was damaged. I told myself not to run the risk of it being sold out elsewhere, and I bought it. It gave me a real jolt. I remember thinking: "Wow, that's incredible!" It made me want to change gears. I felt that I needed to do something completely different from what I had done up to that point."

In the same year that the first chapter of *Domu* was released, Otomo had his very first story published in *Young Magazine*, the magazine in which *Akira* would appear two years later. In *Kanojo no Omoide* aka *Magnetic Rose*, the manga artist once again tackled experimental science fiction, inspired by Kubrick's *2001: A Space Odyssey* (1968). This story, which would later appear as one of three short films in the anthology *Memories* (1995), portrays three astronauts whose deep space freighter is magnetically drawn toward what looks like a gigantic rose made of scrap metal, a chaotic, yet sublime amalgam that Otomo, of course, rendered in painstaking detail. Two of them venture into the maze of steel and find, to their great surprise, Renaissance-style apartments in almost perfect condition. Small robots see to their upkeep, serving their mistress who lies dead on a princess' bed. Reading the woman's diary, the astronauts discover that she was rejected by the man she loved, only to end up isolating herself in this corner of the universe, along with everything she owned. The astronauts flee when the robotic servants start shooting at them, and they escape *in extremis*, before realizing upon take-off that it is the robots who are attracting the scrap metal in order to honor their mistress' love of roses.

In the early eighties, Otomo proved that he was quite comfortable drawing even the most sophisticated of technologies in the domains of robotics, electronics, and aerospace. The astronauts' spaceship in *Kanojo no Omoide,* as well as those in his mini-series *Apple Paradise* (published by *Manga Kisotengai* in 1980), were to inspire an entire generation of artists with whom Otomo's meticulousness had found an echo: "I liked machines. It was as simple as that. I like busy, convoluted stuff." The manga artist submitted another short story, entitled *Buki Yo Saraba* (*A Farewell to Weapons*), to *Young Magazine* in 1981. In it, one can again see the origins of *Akira*, as the tale takes place in a ruined megalopolis and portrays dizzying views from atop the city's dilapidated skyscrapers. A band of soldiers fight a robot, who picks them off one by one. The story ends with the black humor that is so predominant in Otomo's work. The last soldier standing–who has shed his damaged combat suit–is spared by the robot, who doesn't see the naked man as a threat. Filled with despair, the latter then begins to hurl stones at the robot. Otomo's vehicle and combat suit drawings caught the eye of many, so much so that he was actually contacted by a company that wanted to turn them into toys![12] But Otomo wasn't just out to mark the era with his distinctive drawing style, he really wanted to inject a breath of fresh air into the science fiction genre and move beyond *Astro Boy*, *Tetsujin 28-go*, and the other classic manga of his childhood: "As for the mecha design in *A Farewell to Weapons*, Studio Nue's work [*Space Battleship Yamato, Macross*, etc.] was popular at the time, particularly the work of Kazutaka Miyatake and Naoyuki Kato who had drawn some great mechanical suits. But [...], there was no hard-sci-fi manga at the time. I mean, all we had was cute science fiction like *Doraemon*. So, I wanted to change that and do something more realistic and believable. [...] In terms of influences for *A Farewell to Weapons*, [...] well, there were things from *2001: A Space Odyssey* in there as well. Since my work originates in my mind, it means that all my influences are jumbled up and mixed together. My art is shaped by what I've seen, by what I've experienced. I've thus absorbed many different elements from a variety of works over the years. This makes it difficult for me to determine exactly where certain things came from. Simply put, I digest many different elements and ideas that eventually pop up in my work."

And while the year 1982 obviously heralded the birth of *Akira*, Otomo first underwent a formative experience creating, writing, making story-boards and, finally, producing a feature film. The low-budget, buddy film *Jiyu o Warera ni* (a title that plays on the ambiguity of *jiyu*, a word that can mean both gun and freedom, rendering the translated title *Give Us Guns*[13] or *Give Us Freedom*) is about a gang of young gun collectors who wind up fighting on the mountainside after a dispute. Otomo has described this period of his life, stating: "My interest in filmmaking dates back to my high school days. When I was 25, I had a bit of money from my successful manga work. So I spent around 5 million yen to make a 16 mm live-action film that was approximately an hour long. This experience enabled me to study the process of making movies on my own. It gave me a rough idea of how to go about making and directing films."

Although he was initially unaware of it, Otomo's work had already entered the world of cinema a few years earlier, in 1979. One of his stories, *Ninkyo Cinema Club* (published the previous year), served as the screenplay for the erotic comedy *Koko Erotopia Akai Seifuku* directed by

---

12. The prototypes appear in *KABA*, a compilation of Otomo's artwork published in 1989.
13. *KABA* contains a reproduction of the film ticket with the words: "GIVE US GUNS."

Shin'ichi Shiratori. Otomo would have liked to have had a certain degree of control over the project, but this was not to be: "When I read the script and asked if they could rewrite it, they told me the movie was already in the can!" This was also the case with Sogo Ishii's short film *SHUFFLE* (1981), which was based on Otomo's 1979 short story entitled *RUN*, as Ishii never asked Otomo for permission to use his manga. Still, Otomo didn't really hold it against him, as his path and Ishii's fatefully crossed more than once. Ishii wound up directing two other Japanese punk cinema cult films, *Crazy Thunder Road* (1980) and *Burst City* (1982), and the latter laid the foundations for a type of proto-cyberpunk similar to *Akira*, as we will see in an upcoming chapter. And finally, also in 1982, Otomo was entrusted with both the script and the character design for Rintaro's animated feature adaptation of *Harmageddon: Genma Taisen*, a manga co-authored by one of the manga artist's idols, Shotaro Ishinomori. Thus, as he was about to pen the first chapter of *Akira*, Otomo was also working on the adaptation of a tale about psychic powers and the apocalypse... His masterpiece was close at hand and—contrary to what he might have thought at the time—it wouldn't come in the form of a film, but rather in the form of a manga. At least initially.

THE IMPACT OF
AKIRA

A MANGA
[R]EVOLUTION

1.2: Creation: Gestation & Birth

"I wanted to revive a Japan like the one I grew up in after the Second World War, with a government in difficulty, a world being rebuilt, external political pressures, an uncertain future, and a gang of kids left to fend for themselves—even as they cheat boredom by racing on motorbikes."

Katsuhiro Otomo [1]

Given Otomo's insatiable longing for new experiences, he would have undoubtedly found the idea of penning an eight-year-long manga series both too constraining and too tiresome. Back then, no one knew that *Akira* would revolutionize the manga genre, creating a demand for Japanese comics that extended well beyond the country's borders. Nevertheless, Otomo's epic work divided the world of manga into a before and an after, with *Akira* seen as a fundamental break in the history of the medium, both artistically and culturally. And it was a large-scale break indeed. According to *Asahi Shinbun*, a long-standing, widely read, and respectable Japanese daily newspaper, the "Cool Japan" concept would never have come into being if it were not for *Akira*. It was this work's international cultural influence that radically changed Japan's image in the collective consciousness and signaled the emergence of a new Japonism, one that replaced traditional prints with Hello Kitty products.

Akira's modest origin certainly did not foreshadow its remarkable destiny. At the time, the relatively new *Young Magazine*, created by Kodansha in June 1980, was looking for authors to supplement its ranks and give it immediate credibility. Otomo's style and growing fame made him a potential recruit, as the magazine was targeting a "young" core audience, as indicated by its name. Although the magazine's publishers approached him repeatedly, Otomo was already in high demand elsewhere. He was particularly busy working on a lengthy series for *Manga Action*. Based on a story by the novelist Toshihiko Yahagi, it was entitled *Kihun wa mo Senso*, aka *The Mood is Already that of War*. The manga artist was thus struggling to find time to take on additional projects. In fact, 1980 was

1. Paul Gravett. *Comic Heroes Magazine*. no. 19, July 2013.

his most productive year in terms of panel illustrations, as he published a total of 553! And yet, while a new series was out of the question, he could more easily fit short stories into his jam-packed schedule. Otomo thus agreed to produce three short mangas for *Young Magazine*: *Kanojo no Omoide*, aka *Magnetic Rose* (1980), and *A Farewell to Weapons* (1981) as we have previously seen, as well as *Suika Meshia* (*Watermelon Messiah*, 1981), a short work that was highly experimental due to its use of bright colors and lack of script. In it, a giant watermelon crashes into a post-apocalyptic setting, and the inhabitants–looking very much like a colony of ants–rush to retrieve the pieces. As in *Flower* (1979), one can clearly feel Moebius' influence in the silent narration and explosion of color. Finally, in 1982, Otomo also wrote *Dog Afternoon* (1982) for *Young Magazine*, although the illustrations were done by Akihito Takadera.[2]

Speed, a story about music (and musicians) was published in *Just Comic* in February, and it was pretty much the only "major" Otomo publication of 1982. It was a short, twenty-five-page story that resembled his previous body of work, as the manga artist's mind was already elsewhere. He was planning on abandoning his drawing table for six months in order to make the film *Jiyu o Warera ni*. It was almost the end of the year before he was ready to return to manga, agreeing to attend a working meeting with *Young Magazine*'s editors. The idea of a series, a real one this time, was then put on the table. Otomo's recent successes with *Fireball* and especially *Domu* suggested that there was a large audience for this new type of science fiction, and Otomo was asked to continue on in this vein.

Initially, the new series was supposed to be comprised of about ten chapters, which seems absurd in hindsight. This never fails to amuse Otomo (as *Akira* ultimately wound up being one hundred and twenty chapters long). Once again, the manga artist called upon his wealth of ideas, steeped in memories, influences, and past experiences, drawing on them–sometimes unconsciously–to create the sum of parts that would make up *Akira*. Otomo had already paid homage to Osamu Tezuka in *Fireball* (via the ATOM supercomputer) and to Shotaro Ishinomori in *Domu* (via little Etsuko, aka Ecchan). One last great author of Otomo's childhood remained to be saluted in his work: Mitsuteru Yokoyama, the genius behind *Tetsujin 28-go*. Not only did Otomo borrow names from this work, he also appropriated a certain number of ideas, including the discovery of a secret weapon that was supposed to remain buried in the past. In *Tetsujin 28-go*, the weapon in question is a giant robot

---

2. A story that would constitute the first third of the compilation *Sultan Hoeitai*, published in France (by Kana) in 2011 under the name *La Garde du Sultan*.

who is eventually unearthed by a young boy named Shotaro Kaneda, accompanied by his mentor, Dr. Shikishima, whose son is named Tetsuo. Thus, not only did Otomo name three of his main characters after those in Yokoyama's tale, he also made the young titular character (Akira) test subject number 28 in a government experiment. As for the name itself, Akira was not necessarily a nod to Akira Kurosawa as is often claimed, but rather the result of wanting to use a popular Japanese name. Besides honoring another series from his childhood, Otomo was looking to anchor his manga in a given moment: "I also wanted to depict the later Showa period (postwar Japan), including preparations for the Olympics, rapid economic growth, and the student unrest of the 1960s. I was hoping to recreate the assorted elements that built this era in order to craft an exciting story that would seem realistic."

While *Akira* is generally considered cyberpunk, a science fiction subgenre that emerged in the early 1980s, Katsuhiro Otomo's manga actually preceded the work that is considered its defining masterpiece, namely William Gibson's novel *Neuromancer*, by two years. Literature nevertheless had its own echo in *Akira*, as Otomo has cited the influence of novelist Seishi Yokomizo's short stories, some of which appeared serialized in *Weekly Shonen Magazine*. Otomo's youth was marked by the student rebellions of the late 1960s and the emergence of a counterculture embodied in gangs, especially in the *bosozoku* subculture which consisted of bikers like those found in *Akira*.

Ridley Scott's cult film *Blade Runner* came out in movie theaters a few months prior to the release of *Akira*'s first chapter. Otomo has confirmed its influence, not only because the two works have thematic similarities, but also because of Moebius' impact on both artistic endeavors. The iconography and general aesthetics of *Blade Runner*'s 2019 Los Angeles (incidentally, *Akira* was also set in 2019) bear the French artist's mark. Although he did not directly participate in Scott's project, he was offered the role of pre-production assistant. He ultimately declined in order to help with the writing and design of the animated film *Les Maîtres du Temps* by René Laloux (who directed the legendary *Gandahar* five years later), a decision he later said he regretted. Ridley Scott and Moebius had already worked together on the first *Alien* film, another masterpiece celebrated for its set design. One could feel the influence of the cult magazine *Métal Hurlant*, the comics *The Long Tomorrow* and *The Incal* (based on a script by Alejandro Jodorowsky) being among the film's main graphic inspirations. Scott has lauded Moebius' work and the future he depicted in *The Long Tomorrow*: "His work on that was marvelous because he created a tangible future. If the future is one you can see and touch, it makes you a little uneasier because you feel like it's just around the corner."

This "future of tomorrow" had an even greater impact on *Akira*, given the similar language used by Otomo and Moebius: that of the comic strip. The very first panels of *The Long Tomorrow* literally plunge the reader into an urban hell of disconcerting perspectives, where houses, balconies, shops, and roads overlap in what looks more like an anthill than a city. This type of anxiety-provoking gigantism is apparent in *Akira*'s Neo-Tokyo and the chaotic jumble of its concrete monstrosities, twinkling with thousands upon thousands of lights. And for a manga artist as meticulous as Otomo, the idea of an overcrowded and labyrinthine megalopolis couldn't be more appealing. Fritz Lang's film *Metropolis* (1927) also served as one of the inspirations for Neo-Tokyo, particularly in terms of its viewing angles, which showed a resolutely vertical city. These similarities are particularly noticeable in the film *Akira*'s introductory scene. It comes as no surprise that, like Otomo, Lang was a great admirer of Bruegel and his *Tower of Babel*. Otomo even recognized Tokyo in Lang's architectural hodgepodge: "When I first came to Tokyo, I was fascinated by the Ueno district. It was like being in a different era, the post-war period maybe. There were all these old shops lined up on the railway platform. I love dirty, messy places like that. They're nothing like my hometown. [...] Come to think of it, I suppose I enjoy places that are rife with humanity precisely because they lack artificiality. When I was working on the set of *Akira*, I often visited a Tokyo Bay warehouse. Its walls were badly cracked and there were rusty old pipes sticking out all over the place. It was great! And Tokyo itself is messy like that: it's incongruous, completely devoid of artifice. You might suddenly find a Spanish-style villa smack dab in the middle of traditional Japanese architecture. Some people find that sort of thing ugly, but I think such places are fascinating..." In his essay entitled *Transpacific Cyberpunk*, Takayuki Tatsumi—a science-fiction fan and professor at Keio University—went even further. He wrote that, "once the Tokyo Metropolitan Expressway began construction for the convenience of foreign visitors attending the 1964 Olympic Games, we immediately got used to the new atmosphere, appreciating the now ambiguous boundary between the ruins and the construction site. Yesterday's junkyard was immediately transformed into something else altogether. Were it not for this incredible memory, I would have shunned the cyberpunk of the early 1980s."[3] Like Tatsumi (who is only one year younger), Otomo also felt the impact of the 1964 Olympic Games and the popular excitement surrounding them, which explains the presence of an Olympic Stadium

---

3. Takayuki Tatsumi. "Transpacific Cyberpunk: Transgeneric Interactions between Prose, Cinema, and Manga." *Arts*, 7, no. 1, March 2018.

in *Akira*, as well as its symbolic importance, that of a country preparing to celebrate its rebirth.

The motorcycle gang that was to drive *Akira*'s plot was the result of a triple influence. The first was, of course, the *bosozoku*: the youthful motorcycle gangs whose paths Otomo frequently crossed. At the time of *Akira*'s release, they were at the height of their popularity (as their ranks had swelled to 42,500 members). The second was *Mad Max*, especially its sequel *The Road Warrior*, released in 1981. In addition to the thugs astride their bikes, it was the latter's guerrilla atmosphere and gang rivalry that inspired the fights on the streets of Neo-Tokyo, especially those in the impressive opening scene of the 1988 film adaptation. And finally, Otomo was fascinated by Stanley Kubrick's depiction of gratuitous and uninhibited violence in *A Clockwork Orange* (1971).

Otomo thus wanted to portray marginal youth, with his characters looking up at the Neo-Tokyo skyscrapers like insects looking up at giants. The theme of social exclusion was particularly embodied in the character of Tetsuo: "In the story, Tetsuo is on drugs. He becomes so self-destructive that he loses himself. Young people go berserk on impulse and eventually destroy themselves. It's about motorcycle gangs, rock musicians, and punk rockers. You know, those who typically die young. I wanted it to be about the marginal members of society. Outsiders, those who don't belong, are always the most interesting subjects to draw. Young people today must find their own way, like we did. It's not up to us to point the way. They wouldn't listen to us anyway. That's just the way it goes." Otomo could have ultimately concluded *Akira* on that note, so striking are the winds of freedom blowing at the end of this manga, winds that are more like uncontrollable gusts than harmless breezes.

The manga artist had also considered dividing his work in two—rather early on—with the total destruction of his megalopolis occurring in the middle part of the story. One could already sense his excitement in the painstaking depiction of *Domu*'s ruined landscapes, in those long sequences of explosions and collapses that radically transformed the environment. Here, the ordered symmetry deteriorates into ruinous chaos in the span of just a few pages. Otomo attributes such urges to his love of architecture rather than to some hideous thirst for destruction: "In Tokyo, buildings are continually being torn down and rebuilt (something that also has its origins in real estate laws). It's gotten to the point where you almost always see a building under construction when you take a walk outside. Ever since I depicted a huge apartment complex in *Domu*, I've had a much greater interest in architecture, which made me want to draw more buildings under construction. I'm always riveted by these structures, and it was something I didn't really see much of until I moved to Tokyo.

I've drawn so many buildings in my time that I can instinctively see how one would collapse and what pieces it would break into on its way down. I'm always tempted to draw things that pop into my mind. I've actually written stories just to be able to depict buildings being demolished. Maybe I'm driven to destroy them because I want to fully grasp their underlying structures. It's the same with plastic toy models. After I finish building one, I can't help but want to see it flattened. At any rate, I don't think any artist prior to me put this much effort into drawing buildings. When I draw architecture, I take my time and think it through because that's what I like to do. As a result, certain Japanese critics have compared my approach to that of Monsù Desiderio or Piranesi, but there's no truth to that. I'm interested in their art, of course, but their approach was entirely different. They were depicting the frameworks of ancient structures left abandoned over time, while I'm interested in the exact moment a building collapses."

Otomo spoke of several other influences—some of which were undoubtedly obscure to the non-Japanese audience—during a special lecture he gave in Angoulême in 2016 (one year after receiving the Grand Prix in the French city). Besides Tetsuo's appearance, which was inspired by Sting in The Police's *Synchronicity II* clip, he mentioned Shotaro Ishinomori's *Soshite... Dare mo Inaku natta*, aka *And Then,There Were None*, a manga that Otomo had read as a schoolboy. Structurally speaking, the latter was an original work, since its pages contained different and parallel plots: a double-page spread with four simultaneously running stories (one with children, another with a fighter, a third showing warplanes, and a fourth about the Berlin Wall). It ends in a dramatic finale with an atomic bomb falling on New York and razing the city to the ground. While the ghastly double-page spread showing the catastrophe bears a strong resemblance to the opening of *Akira*, Otomo has said that the similarity was not intentional, at least not on a conscious level. And yet, another of these double-page spreads, consisting of collages of various images, events, characters, and stolen moments, found an echo in one of Otomo's last panels for *Akira*, one depicting Tetsuo's memories as they mingle in an amalgam of chaotic emotions. Otomo finds this echo in his work fascinating, as his memory seems to have seized upon it unawares. The structure of *Akira* did indeed embrace the idea of parallel plots, a consequence of Otomo's decision to forgo a main character: "[*Akira*] doesn't revolve around a single figure. No one person is the main character, yet it is possible for many to be seen as such. All people have drama in their lives, so the plot is simply the intermingling of many personal dramas." The filmmaker Sogo Ishii has explained that he finds a certain musicality in the interweaving of storylines: "There's a jazz band that goes by the name of Weather Report. On their recordings, the main melody emerges first, and then all the musicians begin playing it with great gusto. After a while the bass starts to do something different, and then they all begin to improvise. But the rhythm hangs in there and at the end, just when you think the original form has been lost, that initial melody returns. Maybe composing a plot is a bit like that."

Finally, Kaneda's iconic motorcycle was also the result of a number of tributes to (or borrowings from) cinema and culture in general. The first among these was Peter Fonda's chopper in *Easy Rider*, one of the manga artist's cult film favorites. The machine appealed to Otomo because the driver was seated low to the ground: a dignified and imposing position that perfectly suited Kaneda's leadership status. Otomo took this 1960s bike and added elements from another motorcycle (just as famous in pop culture, if not more so): the one from the movie *Tron* (Steven Lisberger, 1982). Appearing in the film's cyberworld, it is rounder and leaves a luminous trail in its wake, a detail highlighted in the film *Akira*. A final, more obscure influence was the work of the German designer Luigi Colani–hailed as the "design messiah" in Japan. His motorcycle models resemble Kaneda's red bike, the latter having the same wheel size and position. To avoid accusations of plagiarism–since some of these references may have been "too identifiable"–Otomo decided to cover his creation with multiple bumper stickers advertising major brands like Canon (for whom he designed and storyboarded two ads in 1984).

The manga artist, however, remains modest with respect to *Akira*. In a 2005 *L'Express* interview, he went so far as to say: "The illustration work wasn't that great. I was young. Even today, I still draw badly... I never really knew where *Akira* was taking me. Nor did I know how the story would end. I was thinking about manga grammar at the time. How to place the panels. The study of expressions. Speech bubbles. Given the length of the project, I had to experiment and move on. *Akira* allowed me to push readers, to make them read the manga as quickly as possible. It had to be read fast, with readers pausing on only the most important panels. Towards the end, it became monotonous, and I decided that we had to end the series (laughs)." The manga artist had already prioritized rhythm in *Domu*, which he likened to a cinematographic experience. For *Akira*, Otomo really wanted to control the speed at which the reader would move from panel to panel. He was once again influenced by the world of cinema, so much so that he imagined the segmentation and composition of his frames in terms of staging, editing, lighting, etc. In the motorcycle racing scenes, for example, the emphasis is on speed and rapid movement, with long squares and omnipresent motion lines driving the reader forward, daring them to keep up with the vehicles themselves. And the widest panels don't depict shocking action scenes, as they do in American comics. Instead, they are often the most uneventful, most contemplative frames in the piece. This points to the manga artist's love of architectural design and its unrivaled precision. Otomo has always avoided the urge to shock for shock's sake, to make artificial stories for the sake of creating equally artificial emotions.

The first chapter of *Akira* appeared in *Young Magazine* on December 20, 1982. This got the ball rolling, but the manga artist didn't go it alone: he initially hired two assistants, before adding a third, a rare occurrence at the time. Working in his studio known as the Mash Room (a reference to the mushroom cloud, perhaps), Otomo was assisted by Yasumitsu Suetake, who would later join him to work on *Spriggan* (1998), *Metropolis* (2001), and *Steamboy* (2004). His two other assistants were Makoto Shiosaki and Satoshi Takabatake. The latter arrived in 1984 and would also go on to collaborate with the manga artist on future works such as *Roujin Z* (1991), *Metropolis*, and *Steamboy*. When Makoto Shiosaki left in 1985, Otomo recruited another budding talent, suggested by *Young Magazine* following a competition for youthful artists: a young man by the name of Satoshi Kon. Barely in his twenties, the future director (not to mention author) of such masterpieces as *Perfect Blue* (1997), *Millennium Actress* (2001), *Tokyo Godfathers* (2003), *Paranoia Agent* (2004), and *Paprika* (2006) thus made his debut with Otomo and also collaborated with him on subsequent projects, including *World Apartment Horror* (1991), *Roujin Z*, and *Metropolis*. Finally, in Angoulême, Otomo revealed the existence of a final, albeit unofficial, assistant: the manga artist was drawing inspiration from Gustave Doré's illustrations, particularly those that the artist had made for *Don Quixote*!

Nevertheless, an author has his pride, and Otomo was accustomed to working alone, at least before the immense undertaking that was *Akira*: "I think working alone suits me best. I worked as helper when I was younger, but I've never worked as an assistant in a manga studio." The manga artist's insistence on quality, his perfectionism, and the bi-monthly publication rhythm left him little choice, however: "At first, I was producing twenty pages per episode, or around forty pages a month. In terms of production, the first thing I did for each chapter was fully complete the first page, just to get into it. I had to work fast, so I didn't even bother with character pose sketches or anything like that. I just drew directly on the comic page I was submitting to the editors, no do-overs. After one page was done, my assistant used a Rotring pen and a ruler to ink out the lines on the buildings and the rest of the backgrounds. I would work ahead of him, completing the rough draft two days before deadline. I'd spend half a day drawing the characters, then wrap up the buildings, adding dust, cracks, and crevices to the windows to give them a bit of life. We'd finish the final draft at 5:00 a.m. on Sunday, have the characters inked by 7:00 p.m., and then submit the completed chapter at 8:00 a.m. Monday morning." The work was daunting, especially the effort required to draw Neo-Tokyo in all its glory. Once again, dizzying perspectives predominated. As for Otomo's striking depth effects, the artist had this to say: "I prefer worlds that have depth. Manga series are drawn on paper, which makes them appear flat and two-dimensional. Nonetheless, a lot of my illustrations have considerable depth to them. I like drawings like that. Whether I'm working on characters or backgrounds, I'm always working to add more and more depth. I don't just draw what's visible on the surface, I want to show things further in, things seen round the back."

Like many of his colleagues haunted by deadlines, Otomo's frantic schedule led to several sleepless nights in his studio. Nevertheless, the manga artist felt as if he were being treated like a king. His publishers gave him carte blanche in terms of creation, something that would radically change in the coming years, as the relationship between artists and publishers grew increasingly complex: "Back in my day, the relationship wasn't as challenging. Nowadays, publishers are very much involved." In the end, Otomo's efforts paid off. *Akira* rapidly found an audience, and the young *Young Magazine* (no pun intended) saw sales that confirmed the artist's momentum. The first of *Akira*'s six *tankobon* was released in September 1984: 300,000 copies quickly sold, despite the rather high retail price of one thousand yen, a commercial success that garnered the series a Kodansha award for best manga of the year.

From 1985 to 1986, publication ran fairly smoothly, although the chapters became shorter (going from twenty pages to sixteen or seventeen on average). The year 1987 marked the first break in the series. For a year and a half, Otomo finally took some time off to work on other projects, including a short animated film that served as the opening and closing to *Robot Carnival*, an anthology that future *Akira* film collaborators Koji Morimoto, Hiroyuki Kitakubo, and Takashi Nakamura would also participate in. This short film is one of Otomo's most unclassifiable works, bringing to mind the dark humored non-stories that he used to write for *Manga Action*: the inhabitants of a small desert village see a giant mobile building on the horizon (bearing the film's title, *Robot Carnival*). In it, rusty robots are dancing and playing music. While the scene initially looks charming, it isn't long before the party turns into a nightmare. The building starts to launch fireworks, which explode like bombs, before "rolling" over the village, thereby flattening it like a house of cards. In the second part, the contraption gets stuck at the top of a dune. As its gears begin to grind, it collapses and is buried by the sand. A man eventually comes along. Finding a metal sphere in the rubble, he decides to bring it home to his family. It resembles a music box with a little ballerina inside, but as the children begin to marvel at the object, it proves to be a bomb. The latter then explodes to reveal the word "END." It's pure Otomo.

The year 1987 also saw the release of the film *Meikyu Monogatari*, aka *Manie-Manie* (subtitled *Labyrinth Tales* in France). Upon its 1992 release in the United States, it was renamed *Neo Tokyo* so as to ride on the coattails of *Akira*'s success. Based on various short stories by the author Taku Mayumura, it was another anthology, composed of three short films. Otomo directed the last animation of the bunch, *Construction Cancellation Order*. Known in Japan as *Koji Chushi Meirei*, this humorous and creative gem included animation work by Koji Morimoto and Takashi Nakamura. Although *Manie-Manie* was released after *Robot Carnival*, it was nevertheless Otomo's first real experience directing an animated film. The story follows a construction company representative sent to South America to halt work at a construction site after revolutionaries have taken power. The problem is that the workers are all robots who are obviously missing more than one bolt. They have been programmed to finish the job and refuse to obey the new order. Seeing more and more money being thrown out of the window on a project that has become obsolete, the representative takes matters into his own hands and goes off to "attack" the central unit powering the robots. The film ends with an unanswered call from the employee's superiors, informing him that the previous government has regained power and that work on the construction site can be resumed.

In terms of animation quality, *Construction Cancellation Order* set the bar for the subsequent *Akira* film: the scenes were opulent, and the representative's facial expressions would soon be shared by the young bikers of the latter work a year later.

As mentioned above, Otomo prefers to work alone so he can have total control over his artistic creations. Nevertheless, while collaborative projects require a very different approach, he didn't find them at all unpleasant. He actually ended up enjoying his initial forays into film and animation more than he'd anticipated: "It might seem strange, but when I'm all alone and drawing, I often wish I was engaging in collaborative cinematographic work. And when I'm working on a film, I want to go back to my drawing board!" And yet, while such a statement seems to suggest that he's eternally dissatisfied, Otomo sees the advantages of both work styles: "Of course, it's both easier and harder to work alone. There's nothing fabulous about drawing manga. You're both relieved and happy when you're finished, but there's no one to share your joy. When you make a film, you have a party with your crew, and then there's the premiere. You miss all that stuff when all you do is draw manga. But there are also drawbacks to filmmaking. For instance, sometimes it's really difficult to get your ideas across to your crew. Nonetheless, I've discovered the joy in working with other people."

Of course, 1987 was the year that would launch production of the animated adaptation of *Akira*, a project that, at the beginning, was not Otomo's doing, but that of his Kodansha editors. He was offered the project of his dreams: a real animated feature film, total control over its content, and a generous budget to go along with it. Although he was more than happy to accept, there remained two significant problems that could not be ignored. First and foremost, Otomo hadn't even finished his manga series yet. And second, there was the difficult challenge of fitting *Akira*'s plot into a single feature film. On the other hand, his film was to be an adaptation, meaning that he didn't have to be entirely faithful to the manga series. Not only was it wise to cut out certain elements, he knew that it was essential: "I didn't even consider taking the comic version as it was and turning it into animation. I thought of the film as a completely different entity. Seeing as I was the one who wrote the original content, my first thought was to create a separate world for the film. I guess the main issue was the film's length. It's hard to bring everything together inside of two hours. Plus, at that point, I hadn't even written the conclusion. It was rough, knowing that I had to come up with an ending. I had to begin by writing the end."

Cuts to the "original content" were predominately made by leaving out the second half of the manga, which was then ready for publication. Moviegoers would not witness the catastrophic event depicted in the manga version, as a revived Akira razes Neo-Tokyo to the ground, transforming it into a post-apocalyptic hell. This cut served to weed out certain characters, such as Lady Miyako, while reducing the importance of others such as Kaori and Kei. By starting the film with Akira already dead–a surprising anticlimax–Otomo was able to skillfully preempt a number of auxiliary storylines, while reproducing the breathless rhythm of the first half of the series' conclusion and integrating it into the ending he'd chosen. And if the manga, released two years after the film, remains more substantial than its cinematographic version, their essence is more or less the same: Tetsuo turns into an abominable mass of pink flesh, and Akira, whose spirit reappears in the film, intervenes to counter his destructive powers and cart him off to another dimension.

The film adaptation of *Akira* would not be a modest project. While the film's considerable budget played a role in this, the project's scope was largely facilitated by a group of participants who joined forces to form an "*Akira* committee." The latter was composed of Toho (the film distribution company), Kodansha, the Tokyo Movie Shinsha–or TMS–studio (one of the oldest, most prestigious studios in Japan), the Mainichi Broadcasting System, Laserdisc Corporation, the advertising agency Hakuhodo, and Sumitomo Corporation. They were all willing to lend a hand (and open their wallets) to help finance and advertise the film, whose budget exceeded the symbolic one-billion-yen mark (1.1 billion yen to be exact, about 1.3 billion yen in present day terms, translating into roughly twelve million USD). This division of the budget, which reduced individual risk, would become the norm for the Japanese animation industry. Everyone was hoping for a major commercial success on Japanese soil, as this was the primary and essential target, well ahead of export considerations abroad. As is the case with Japanese video games, the country's production is largely geared toward domestic consumption, as this is where most of the demand lies.

Otomo's young animation assistants ultimately proved to be his dream team. In addition to Koji Morimoto, Hiroyuki Kitakubo, and Takashi Nakamura, whom we've previously mentioned, there was also the great Toshiyuki Inoue, a true legend in the world of animation as his resume can attest. His most esteemed projects include *Royal Space Force: The Wings of Honneamise* (1987), *Kiki's Delivery Service* (1989), and later Otomo's *Roujin Z* and *Steamboy* (1991, 2004), *Ghost in the Shell* and its sequel *Innocence* (1995, 2004), *Jin-Roh* (*The Wolf Brigade*, 1999), and *Paprika* (2006). Hideki Hamasu was also part of the team, although his name didn't appear in the credits. It did, however, appear in several Ghibli studio releases as well as Satoshi Kon films, including *Perfect Blue*, *Tokyo Godfathers*, and *Paprika*. And, although most of the team members were relatively young (around thirty years of age), Yoshinori Kanada (credited Kaneda on *Akira*) acted as their patriarch since—"back in the day"—he'd participated in the emergence of the 1970s space opera and mecha wave. The artist had indeed worked on several legendary anime series, including *Uchu Senkan Yamato* (*Space Battleship Yamato*, 1974), *Getter Robo* (1974), *Dino Mech Gaiking* (1976), *Mobile Suit Gundam* (1979), and *Galaxy Express 999* (1978), all well before the making of *Akira*.

The film budget's size was commensurate with the effort and the amount of work the project required. At the height of production, there were nearly seventy people working with Otomo (both day and night) in his studio, many of whom had been motivated by the idea of working with him alone. And this number doesn't even include external contributors, as many artists were borrowed from other studios, including Telecom Animation Film, Dragon Production, Nakamura Production, the great Studio Uni, Studio Fuga, Baku Production, Ishigaki Production, and Kobayashi Production. The demand for quality was constant, and the number of celluloids produced is proof of this: there were 160,000 in total. This wasn't the "limited animation" found on television, which ran at twelve, or even just eight, frames per second. *Akira* ran at twenty-four, hence the astonishing impression of fluidity. And if these numbers aren't enough, the film ended up with 2,212 shots and 327 colors (a record), fifty of which were specially created for the feature film. This last point is apparent if you pay close attention to the lights of Neo-Tokyo as well as the nuances found in the shadows and various backdrops. Chief colorist Kimie Yamana referred to this imperative, saying that the film is set mostly at night and that, "if you look at the color chart, you'll see the tremendous variety of dark tones, many colors you wouldn't see in any other animation. There is such subtlety in the various tones that you wouldn't notice them on a television screen. But in the theater, this wide array of colors really does make a difference." *Akira*'s aesthetics, with its colors and backdrops, would influence an entire culture in the years to come. The short army helicopter scene featuring Takashi and Masaru already depicted the red and magenta hues that we would later find in the aesthetic codes of the eighties and cyberpunk revival. But while Akira represented—and probably still represents—the apogee of traditional animation, Otomo also exploited the fledgling technology of computer animation before anyone else. Most notably, it was used in the film to create Tetsuo and Akira's light energy, as observed by the scientists in their laboratories. Once again, Otomo was the pioneer of an artistic movement, the natural evolution of his medium that he had perceived before anyone else.

All of this work was also necessary to portray Neo-Tokyo's immensity on the big screen. The artistic director, Toshiharu Mizutani, explained: "In order to show the vastness of the city, we had to draw thousands of individual buildings and additional structures, and then, we had to create perspective in order to show depth. For instance, we began with three-millimeter windows on the buildings. Then, the buildings directly behind those were given windows that were only half a millimeter, and those even further back were represented by a dot, or perhaps a line. It required very precise drawing. We had a lot of night scenes, and blue tones are typically used to create that effect. But I tried to use an unorthodox color scheme that stressed reds and greens. It was an experiment that I'd always wanted to try, and Otomo approved."

As in the manga version, Neo-Tokyo had to be an integral part of the plot, a full-fledged character to be both feared and protected. The animated film version gave Otomo the opportunity to present the megalopolis in all its richness. "It's extremely difficult to express the depth of such a vast city. Originally, I used each issue of the manga to build on its depth and size. I created various situations in an attempt to tell the story through graphic images. But with film, every aspect is combined, making it more convincing than a serialized manga, at least in my opinion. A manga or comic is just a picture, while animation allows you to add color, sound, and motion. I felt that I could now create the type of atmosphere I had envisioned for Neo-Tokyo." This motion is even felt in the film's first few minutes, in the broken shots showing a dense forest of massive buildings, illuminated by millions of neon lights, in which it would be easy to lose one's bearings.

As the film's only director, Otomo had full control over the project and produced the entire storyboard in advance. It was comprised of 783 scenes. There was an enormous amount of work involved: "I actually drew every possible scene that could have appeared in the film. Then, I began to cut those that weren't absolutely necessary. That's why the storyboarding for this film took so much time. I think that's the most difficult part of the animation process: you really have to finish your film on the storyboard first. You can't shoot a lot of extra film and then do your edits, like in live action movies. Some editing does indeed take place, but it's normally done just to overlap scenes. I generally pour all of my energy into the storyboarding phase, because I know that it will facilitate production as a whole." But Otomo's biggest challenge wasn't storyboarding the most complex or spectacular scenes; on the contrary, the devil was, as is often the case, in the details: "There were so many simple scenes that presented difficulties, even just having a character walk toward the camera. In television, the camera can just pan to the upper sections, but my film characters' entire bodies needed to be visible, and their movements had to look real. Many seemingly simple scenes ended up giving me the biggest headaches."

But the making of *Akira* wasn't merely the result of the entire animation team's painstaking work. The film also relied on revolutionary tools and techniques, including (at the time) the rather iconoclastic use of pre-recorded voices. Where dubbing usually occurs late in an animated film's production, Otomo shook things up. He insisted that they be recorded beforehand, using only the storyboard. The animators thus had to make the characters' lips move to match the voices, and not the other way around. This gave the actors, many of whom were still unknown to the general public, much more freedom to express themselves, as explained by Kaneda's voice actor Mitsuo Iwata: "It was a first for me. I knew that pre-recording was popular in the United States, especially at Disney. Once I got into it, I felt like I was doing a radio drama; it really lets an actor get into the part and express himself. I was amazed after my first take. I watched the screen and saw the animated character I was portraying. He was talking in my voice: it didn't seem like animation at all." This sentiment was shared by Mami Koyama, the actress who voiced Kei: "I think Otomo is a genius. He didn't give us any directives with respect to the characters, so we had to decide for ourselves how he would want them to sound. It was a true learning experience."

Another process ahead of its time was the Quick Action Recorder. This machine enabled one to consult a computer screen to determine whether the synchronization of sound and image was convincing. While animators used to spend a great deal of time on this, the Quick Action Recorder's preview highlighted inaccuracies much more quickly, saving precious time in terms of retouching, especially if the latter was required once the animation was well underway. The pre-recording, coupled with the Quick Action Recorder, made *Akira*'s dialogue a model of realism and authenticity, and it remains so today.

Finally, *Akira* would not have the cultural influence it enjoys today without its anthology soundtrack. It was Otomo who would choose the composer and, once again, recording preceded animation and editing to promote greater artistic freedom. The director was listening to the album *Ecophony Rinne*, released in 1986, when he chose the Geinoh Yamashirogumi collective to compose and perform *Akira*'s music. The choice was both astonishing and risky, and many of Otomo's colleagues were skeptical, if not downright apprehensive. Geinoh Yamashirogumi is a collective of amateur musicians united around its brilliant founder, Shoji Yamashiro, whose real name is Tsutomu Ohashi. Like those in his collective, Yamashiro is not a professional musician; he is in fact a scientist, having received a Doctorate of Agriculture. But to reduce Yamashiro to a diploma or label would lack respect. He is, above all, incorrigibly curious, an enlightened explorer of sound forever in search of novelty. Some might even call him a bit eccentric. Yamashiro combines his interest in music with that of anthropology, biology, artificial life, and Kansei engineering (a field that links the creation of products to the psychological and emotional needs of their users). Although the collective's first album was released in 1976 (*Osozeran/Do no Kenbai*, which opens with a shrill scream), we have to go back to 1953 to find the origin of the group. It was a simple band of students from various universities who came together to form a mixed choir. Yamashiro took over its direction in 1966 and finally gave the group its definitive name in 1974. Being interested in all types of music, the composer took his troupe to various countries in search of new musical experiences. The collective's discography thus features many different styles, from Bulgarian chant (*Chi no Hibiki: Higashi Yoroppa wo Utau*, aka *Reverberation of Earth*, 1976) to African music (*Africa Genjo*, 1982), not to mention rock fusion and traditional Japanese music and *noh* [a traditional Japanese drama featuring dance and song]. And that's not all: Geinoh Yamashirogumi has also organized an annual festival in the heart of Shinjuku since the mid-1970s. Based on kecak (pronounced [*kechak*]), a Bal͏͏͏͏ese hindu celebration combining dance, theater, and song, it is acco͏͏͏panied by the sounds of traditional instruments like the gamelan. ͏͏͏re ever lucky enough to pass through the area during the festival, ͏͏͏owerful male choruses and the tinkling of the gamelan will inevitably remind you of *Akira*'s soundtrack. When he heard that Otomo had selected him and his band, Yamashiro was astounded: "To be honest, my first reaction was 'Why me?' Mr. Otomo had even asked if it was possible to use one of my old albums, *Ecophony Rinne*. I was stunned. Mr. Otomo was free to choose anyone he liked, and yet he wanted to use my music, even if it meant recycling a preexisting work. That's the primary reason I agreed to collaborate with him. It meant that, in Mr. Otomo's mind, Geinoh Yamashirogumi was the only possible choice: I couldn't refuse." But even though Otomo was sure of his choice, there was no guarantee that Yamashiro would agree to compose new music for his feature film. The director thus approached him cautiously, initially suggesting limited involvement: "I told him that we could manage if he just wrote two new pieces for the feature film. But I only said that to convince him to work with us. Although I said that I only wanted two tracks, I really needed a lot more. When I showed him all the rush animations and storyboards, Yamashiro fell in love with the story. He ended up composing the entire film score."

Geinoh Yamashirogumi is a musical laboratory in and of itself. An entity in constant fluctuation, it perhaps owes its insatiable thirst for novelty to the fact that many of its members work in scientific circles. The collective even hosts two internal organizations, the Festival Arts Research Institute and the Civilization Sciences Research Institute. Both of these organizations act as pioneers in the search for new musical styles, and some of their members travel the earth to bring back local oddities. The band masters nearly eighty instruments in all, and its impressive sound diversity can be heard throughout its discography.

When Otomo heard *Ecophony Rinne*, he knew he had found the sound he wanted for *Akira*, and the similarities between the album and the film soundtrack were ultimately striking. This is true not only in terms of style but also in terms of theme. *Ecophony Rinne* had the particularity of being constructed around three movements representing the cycle of birth, death, and rebirth. This echoes *Akira*'s themes, especially the metaphysical dimension of its last act. Yamashiro and his musicians have infused it with a mystical, primal energy that combines the brutal and the spiritual, mixing wild roars with sibylline choruses. The total freedom granted by Otomo can be found in the variety of instruments used, including the jegog (a Balinese percussion instrument with a distinctive sound) and the gamelan (used at kecak festivals), all of which are obviously carried by the choruses, whether they are male, female, Bulgarian, or *noh-style*. The human voice is actually the most beautiful instrument in the collective.

Geinoh Yamashirogumi also enjoyed an unlimited budget for the project. And there were no limits on the collective's artistic freedom either, as Otomo understood that the composer's genius (and that of his collaborators) was based on forgoing convention. Any directives would only hinder their insatiable curiosity. And Otomo went even further in terms of artistic license, since he asked Yamashiro not to compose a film soundtrack as such—the editing wasn't finished yet anyway—but to instead to give full rein to his inspiration and compose music that would fit Neo-Tokyo's atmosphere, in the style of Geinoh Yamashirogumi. He then intended to draw from the band's compositions to set the music for his film, as he explained by once again referencing a beloved director: "Stanley Kubrick often uses preexisting music, so I asked Mr. Yamashiro to compose a stand-alone piece instead of cheerful or creepy accompaniments designed to fit scenes. I wanted to take the piece and use sections from it as we saw fit." Things weren't that simple, of course: composing original tracks without being able to rely on a scene's rhythm or tone can be lethal for the artistic coherence of a work and one's immersion in a feature film. If image and sound fail to complement one another, both will suffer. Yamashiro avoided this pitfall by adopting a very particular method of composition. He created "modules," i.e. musical units that could be combined as desired to form movements of adjustable duration. The composer also used sample-based synthesizers to adapt the sound of the gamelan to a particular scale. This made it easier to deconstruct his compositions and integrate them into the feature film without the cuts being too noticeable. Nevertheless, Yamashiro wasn't entirely happy with the results. A true sound enthusiast, the composer struggled to transcribe his art using the sound technology available at the time. Stereo wasn't enough to create the movement or density desired by Yamashiro, who wanted to sublimate the richness of the images with music that would blend into the environment and be an integral part of it.

It wasn't until 2001, with the emergence of surround sound and 5.1 technology, that Yamashiro was finally able to bring his true vision to life. The re-release of *Akira* in Japanese movie theaters in 2002, as well as its release in DVD format, brought a new dimension to Otomo's film, something that Hideo Takada, the remastering sound engineer, recalls vividly: "I think [the multitrack] is a key element in Geinoh Yamashirogumi's musical creations. When you inject several musical essences into a single piece of music, you see possibilities that you hadn't even thought of. Different musical elements intertwine, confront each other, blend together. And with all these elements, multitrack audio becomes very effective in expressing just about anything. I think it has its own lyrical form, which turns the music into a kind of message. That's why *Akira* should be listened to in multitrack, and not in two channels. It best expresses the sound that its composer was going for."

The difference was so great that it overwhelmed Otomo. Indeed, the director experienced a certain bitterness when his feature film was originally released in 1988: "When I saw the premiere of the film version of *Akira*, I thought it was a failure. I left the theater quickly and came back home to tell my wife that it would be a flop. While I thought that the first half was good, I felt that the quality plummeted as the story developed, mostly due to all the cuts we'd made due to time and budget constraints. [...] However, when Shoji Yamashiro did the remake with five-channel audio, he invited me over and showed it to me. I hadn't seen the film since its release, so a lot of time had passed. Maybe that made me softer, but when I saw it again, I thought, 'Oh, this is interesting, maybe it wasn't so bad after all.'"

And, as history has confirmed, the film wasn't "so bad after all." As of its release on July 16, 1988, *Akira* met with enormous success in Japan, where it eventually grossed more than six times its budget (or 6.35 billion yen). And Otomo wasn't yet finished with Kaneda, Tetsuo, and the rest of the gang, since the manga version of his work remained unfinished. It took him nearly two more years to complete the series: the final, one hundred and twentieth chapter, appeared in the pages of *Young Magazine* on June 25, 1990. However, many consider *Akira*'s true ending as the sixth and last *tankobon*, released in March 1993, since Otomo added several dozen pages to further develop his ending. He even went so far as to modify old drawings, a practice that was common to both Otomo and his colleagues, as the rhythm of publication obviously entailed both haste and a number of cuts which were then rectified in the *tankobons*. And indeed, these were often the versions that served as source material for publication abroad. At this point, the manga artist was so worn out that he was hard-pressed to finish his work. A lingering rumor even suggests that it was the Franco-Chilean director and comic strip writer Alejandro Jodorowsky who helped Otomo come up with *Akira*'s ending. Surprisingly, this rumor has been confirmed by Otomo himself! Jodorowsky tells the story as he remembers it: "Otomo says this, but I have no memory of it (laughs). During a *Santa Sangre* screening in Tokyo, I was told that I could have lunch with the artist of my choice. They were surprised when I asked if I could meet Otomo. We met in a Chinese restaurant over a bottle of whiskey, accompanied by a geisha. Otomo started drinking and, although I never drink, I joined him out of politeness. I quickly became drunk. Otomo said he was having trouble coming up with an ending for *Akira*. After that, all I know is that I grabbed a pencil and scribbled something out. But I can't for the life of me remember what it was (laughs)."

But let's rewind just a bit. While the film also enjoyed a certain degree success in the West, at least among the initiated, Americans had first benefited from the manga version, or rather a "special" manga version, before the feature film was even released in movie theaters. Indeed, the edition published by Epic Comics (an imprint of Marvel) had the singularity of being entirely colorized. It also read from left to right, as opposed to the Japanese version which read from right to left. We have to return to the early eighties to find the origin of this unlikely collaboration. Yasumasa Shimizu, from Kodansha, offered the following explanation: "I first visited New York, accompanied by Katsuhiro Otomo, in 1983. We had a meeting with Archie Goodwin, who was then the Editor-in-Chief at Marvel. He was working on *Spider-Man* at the time. He said that he had seen *Akira* and really wanted to publish it. Otomo-*sensei* didn't want *Akira* to be perceived as 'something bizarre from Japan,' so we worked hard to make it accessible to American audiences. That kind of effort would be unimaginable today, but at the time, we rendered it in all color and flipped the artwork to be read from left-to-right (as is the Western style). When you flip manga artwork, the images end up shifting a little, making them look a bit off. So, Otomo-*sensei* made adjustments to the flipped artwork, and these changes are specific to the American version. He's a huge fan of French and American comics. He thought he had the potential to become a world-renown artist, so it was very important to him to have his work understood and perceived as international. Otomo-*sensei* really enjoyed having fans from all over the world, and as editors, we wanted to help him grow his fan base."

According to Steve Oliff, who was the colorist for *Akira* from 1988 onwards, Otomo believed that the American public wasn't ready for "raw" black and white manga, since readers were accustomed to colorful, flashy comic strips. The collaboration between Oliff and Otomo was thus both close and longstanding. And, despite the language barrier, the two men had no problems communicating with one another. In February 2016, Oliff posted a video detailing their initial meeting on *YouTube*: "I first met Otomo after flying into New York. [He and his editors] liked my samples the best, and they offered me the job. Otomo didn't say much, but his English improved when we went out to grab some sushi and sake and knock back a few beers. I found out later that his spoken English was a lot better than he let on." Trust between the two men—one Japanese and the other American—grew from there. The manga artist also visited Oliff's home in Point Arena, California to discuss the color adaptation. Otomo had even started coloring in the first few pages of a personal copy to give Oliff an idea of what he wanted! The two artists thus established the basics for the adaptation over a bottle of Jack Daniels. In 1998, Oliff began sending his work to Kodansha so that it could be approved before its release on the American market. Otomo personally approved the first five episodes. He then concluded that Oliff was on the right track, and allowed the colorist to submit his work directly to Epic Comics: "They sent me really high-quality copies from Japan, which allowed me to use airbrush, colored pantone film, paint, colored pencils, felt pens... any medium that I wanted to try. The paper held up to it all, and I was able to do fully painted color guides." The main source of inspiration for the manga colorization was supposed to be the *Akira* film, but Oliff began working on the project before the movie was even released. To help the colorist get off on the right foot, Otomo sent him slides of the feature film in progress.

Oliff and his studio, Olyoptics, worked on *Akira*'s colorization from 1988 to 1994, finishing their work four years after the manga's final serialization in Japan. The colorist has said that the last volumes could have been published more quickly, but Otomo took some time off to work on his next major project, the film *Steamboy*, which would eventually be released in 2004. Archie Goodwin and the Kodansha staff had agreed on a different publication format for Otomo's manga series. Rather than publishing over one hundred chapters of about twenty pages each, they had decided that Epic Comics would publish thirty-eight volumes, each comprised of sixty-four pages. *Akira* also marked another turning point in the comic book industry. Oliff and his team persuaded Marvel to use digital coloring, and the series became the first ongoing comic book to be colorized this way, using a PC with a 12-megahertz processor and a handmade heat diffuser that chugged like a farm tractor! And despite the rudimentary technology, real progress was being made in the field. Otomo's work was once again spearheading a new movement: "*Akira* triggered a big change in the industry. After a while, it even changed people's expectations in terms of color. Our motto at Olyoptics is 'the better you draw, the better we color.' Otomo's designs made everyone up their game. [...] *Akira* changed the history of comics. A lot of people still tell me how important it was to them, how different it looked at the time." There was, of course, no guarantee that Americans would come to appreciate this new genre of comic book, with its entirely different artistic and narrative codes. But perhaps it was this attraction to the unfamiliar that made all the difference. In his article "Manga Goes Global," Jean-Marie Bouissou suggests a possible explanation for the foreign success of *Akira*, as well as manga in general, in the 1980s: "Manga finally cracked the US market open in 1987-1988.[4] One cannot help but notice the concomitance with two phenomena. In 1985, the Plaza Accord pushed the yen up by almost 75%. A flurry of Japanese investment abroad immediately followed. This onslaught fueled a forceful

---

4. *Akira* was not the first manga to appear in the US, since First Comics had imported *Lone Wolf and Cub* by Kazuo Koike & Goseki Kojima one year before, while Eclipse et Viz Comics had published *Kamui* by Sanpei Shirato.

Japan-bashing trend in the US and also in France, albeit to a lesser degree. Media turned the heat on the Japanese, and hate-books appeared on the shelves, including revealing titles such as *The Coming War With Japan*. The manga boom is closely linked to this conjuncture."[5] Could manga have represented a counterculture? Isn't our interest in a work piqued when it is demonized or suppressed? In any case, the Americanized version of *Akira* was a resounding success, both in terms of public reception and professional recognition. Steve Oliff won the best colorist award for *Akira* in 1992–an award that he also won in 1993 and 1994–and this was before the color version had even been published in Japan! And once "manga mania" was well established, Americans were finally able to rediscover Otomo's manga in its original black and white form. The series, published by Dark Horse Comics, ran in the US from 2000 to 2002.

Akira was also a bombshell success in France. The French context differed to a certain extent: France had already gotten a taste of Japanese animation in the form of several anime exported as early as the late 1960s. Among these were *Goldorak* (*UFO Robot Grendizer*, aka *Force Five: Grandizer*), the 1978 *Candy* (*Candy Candy*), and *Uchu kaizoku Captain Harlock* (*Albator, le corsaire de l'espace*, aka *Space Pirate Captain Harlock*). Of course, these anime had a different–less violent–tone than did *Akira* (with their more serious passages being removed or rewritten via censorship). They were thus often categorized as children's programs. This is where *Akira* faced a real challenge: in both the United States and France, cartoons were still irrevocably associated with children, and the idea of animation for adults, even young adults, was considered laughable, an oddity. Almost a deception. And, while the characters on these televised series rapidly entered into pop culture, they didn't trigger a manga boom. The few magazine adaptations that were released only enjoyed limited success, with the possible exception of *Candy Candy Poche*, in 1982. All previous attempts to export real manga had ended in failure. Beginning in 1978, Atoss Takemoto and his magazine *Le Cri qui tue* had tried to share the works of Osamu Tezuka, Shotaro Ishinomori, and Yoshihiro Tatsumi, but the audience just wasn't there. In 1983, the publishing house Les Humanoïdes Associés (founded by Moebius among others) also tried to introduce manga to the French market with the first volume of *Barefoot Gen* (*Hadashi no Gen*), but to no avail, most likely due to the very Japanese subject matter. (Les Humanoïdes Associés went on to publish *Domu*, renamed *Rêves d'Enfants*, aka *The Dreams of Children*, in 1991).

5. Jean-Marie Bouissou. "Manga Goes Global." *Critique Internationale*, vol. 7, 2000, Culture Populaire et Politique, edited by Denis-Constant Martin, pp. 1-36.

It was only when *Akira* came out that something finally clicked. In 1988, Jacques Glénat (founding president of Glénat Editions) went to Japan to present his catalog. There, he discovered the manga culture and the phenomenon that was *Akira*. Seeing a certain resemblance between Otomo's work and the Franco-Belgian comic strip genre, Glénat decided to negotiate publishing rights with Kodansha, talks that lasted nearly a year. During this time, French bookshops that offered American comics in their original version also began to sell the Americanized version of *Akira*, which caught the eye of connoisseurs. And it was this colorful version that Glénat initially sought to publish, as he feared that the classic black and white manga would seem too archaic alongside the bright colors of Franco-Belgian and American comics. And so, in partnership with the newspaper *Libération*, Glénat published the first French issue of *Akira*, which appeared in newsstands on March 15, 1990. And although its initial success was moderate at best–Glénat even called it a total flop–the film's release in France on May 8, 1991 (which garnered 100,000 admissions, including 40,000 in the Paris region), coupled with the release of the first hardback volumes that same year, would considerably boost the success of the Otomo series, and thus launch "manga mania": a force that nothing could stop, even as an alarmed generation of adults denounced the arrival of such comics and called them every name in the book. Thumbing his nose at the manga detractors and the constant threat of censorship, Glénat came up with an accurate and provocative slogan to promote *Akira*: "It's violent, and it's beautiful."

THE IMPACT OF
AKIRA

A MANGA
[R]EVOLUTION

1.3: Creation: Maturity

A *KIRA* WILL UNDOUBTEDLY REMAIN OTOMO'S career-defining master-piece. Not only did he dedicate eight years of his life to this pivotal work, it almost certainly took a toll on his health as well. It is rare for an artist, even one of his caliber, to come out with a second ground-breaking work of the same magnitude, one that might eventually come to rival the legendary status of the first. After *Akira*, Otomo more or less abandoned manga. His professional projects were few and far between, in sharp contrast to the first twenty years of his career and its intense output.

And yet, it is not entirely true that he gave up on manga altogether. While Otomo no longer took on enormous illustrative projects like *Akira*, he did write the storyline for *The Legend of Mother Sarah*, a manga whose images were drawn by Takumi Nagayasu. It appeared (rather sporadically) in *Young Magazine* from 1990 to 2004 and was published by Dark Horse Comics (in the United States) and Delcourt (in France). The background is similar to that of *Space Battleship Yamato* and *Mobile Suit Gundam*: nuclear warfare has rendered Earth uninhabitable, and most of humanity has taken refuge in various satellite colonies. A scientist eventually proposes the use of a "clean" bomb to change the Earth's axis of rotation. This could restore the planet's southern hemisphere while burying its northern one under a mound of ice and snow. The proposition subsequently leads to a conflict between a pro-bomb faction and an anti-bomb faction. The resulting terrorism forces the colonists to return to Earth. These are, of course, classic post-war manga themes.

In 1991, Otomo wrote another script, this time for an animated film: the hilarious *Roujin Z*, directed by his colleague Hiroyuki Kitakubo. In it, Otomo uses satire to tackle the difficult subject of the aging Japanese population's isolation, which he had previously touched upon in *Domu*. *Roujin Z* tells the story of an unfortunate eighty-seven-year-old patient who is "volunteered" to test a new ultra-computerized "smart bed" that will supposedly meet all his needs. The bed in question is powered by a small nuclear reactor. It thus comes as little surprise that the bed is actually a top-secret government weapon. The self-sustaining device ultimately destroys a good portion of the city in a crescendo of gleeful violence. Although the tone of the piece is radically different than that of *Akira*, the two works have a number of common themes. That same year, the manga artist directed a new live-action film entitled *World Apartment Horror*.

Based on a story by Satoshi Kon, the screenplay was written by Otomo and the young screenwriter Keiko Nobumoto, who would eventually become famous for her work on *Cowboy Bebop*. More of a comedy than a horror film, *World Apartment Horror* thrusts a *yakuza* mobster into a small community of immigrants. He is tasked with evicting them from their shabby apartments, but cultural and linguistic barriers get in the way. The situation is further complicated by the evil spirit that appears to haunt the building. It was not Otomo's best film, but even *Roujin Z* wasn't of *Akira*'s caliber (nor should we have expected it to be) despite the advertising campaigns that lauded Otomo's work. Both films were later adapted into manga: Satoshi Kon wrote *World Apartment Horror*, which appeared in *Young Magazine*, while Tai Okada penned *Roujin Z,* renamed *ZeD,* for *Mister Magazine*.

Otomo's feature length film *Memories* (1995) is an anthology composed of three of his short stories. The first, *Kanojo no Omoide* (aka *Magnetic Rose*), is an adaptation of a manga published fifteen years earlier in *Young Magazine*. Koji Morimoto directed the short, while Satoshi Kon served as screenwriter and artistic director. Not only is it the longest of the three shorts, it is, by far, the best: an excellent adaptation of the original content. The second, *Stink Bomb*, directed by Tensai Okamura, is somewhat less intriguing, while the last, *Cannon Fodder*, is the most experimental. Directed by Otomo himself, it consists of a twenty-minute continuous shot depicting an industrial city where cannons are as widespread as the military propaganda that celebrates them. The absurdity of war is once again highlighted in this latter work, as is so often the case in Otomo's manga. *Memories* also marked a change in the director's way of doing things, which evolved with the times: "When I worked on *Memories*, my team used computer graphics for animation. This was particularly true at the beginning of *Cannon Fodder*, when the young boy is running down the hallway. That part was made using CG animation. So, it was a 3D model of the corridor, and it was composited with 2D animation. Originally, we tried to do it with a composite of live-action footage, but the quality wasn't very good, so we switched to CG. The sequence worked really well, so much so that Koji Morimoto wanted to use it for his piece *Magnetic Rose*. [...] After we wrapped up *Memories*, we thought about doing a lot more with CG. Not only did I think about using this type of animation much more frequently, I really tried to figure out the best way to use the technology."

With the year 2000 just around the corner, Otomo continued working, this time writing the screenplay for the animated feature film adaptation of *Metropolis*, a manga by Osamu Tezuka, which allowed him to pay tribute to one of his childhood heroes in a fitting manner. Although the film (directed by Rintaro and released in 2001) was only loosely based on the original work, they nevertheless shared the same concerns, namely total destruction, the difficult question of identity, and social—even racial—segregation. And Otomo was able to satisfy his destructive bent yet again: "I liked seeing the perfect city get destroyed in the end. It was thrilling." Widely praised by critics, the film was nevertheless a commercial failure, earning only three-quarters of its original budget of one billion yen. But Otomo wasn't yet finished with Tezuka: his next film, *Steamboy*, was based on the famous *Astro Boy*. In 1994, the director had been planning to make a simple three-episode OVA series with a budget of 300 million yen, an amount that quadrupled in 1997 with the support of Bandai. It took almost ten years to make what eventually became a new large-scale animated film. During this decade, Otomo was plagued by financing problems that forced him to approach Hollywood, but negotiations with James Cameron, Roland Emmerich, and producer Joel Silver came to naught, since Otomo did not want to compromise his artistic freedom. The film was already well underway in the early 2000s. To save it and avoid crippling financial losses, several Japanese companies, including Toho, Sony Pictures, the studio Sunrise (which would finish production), Bandai Visual, and Production I.G., dug their wallets out and *Steamboy* was finally released in the movie theaters in 2004. Far from enjoying *Akira*'s success, Otomo's *Steamboy* did not even recoup its colossal budget of 1.8 billion yen.

It wasn't a bad film, far from it. In terms of substance, it may have lacked *Akira*'s visceral and uncompromising tone, but *Steamboy* had graphic qualities that critics definitely noticed in the midst of the computer animation boom. And this was not a foregone conclusion because, as Otomo later explained, the film's production met with delay after delay, while technological advances continued on: "The delays were unfortunate. When *Steamboy* was finally released, the CG animation was no longer cutting edge." Even so, the steampunk aesthetics of nineteenth century England were magnificent, and the film's backdrops were bursting with all the detail of Otomo's prior works: "That era has always fascinated me. I worked hard to recreate the true texture of the nineteenth century in all its detail, right down to the viscous appearance of the oil, the heat and humidity of the steam, and the rust of the metal. To achieve that level of realism, everything was first drawn by hand and then combined with digital technology to incorporate special effects. This is how I was able to create an authentic, intense universe for the story." The narrative in question returns to the main themes of Otomo's work, or at least those that he prefers to address in science fiction, i.e. the dangers associated with the misuse of science, war, youth and the hope it represents, etc. He wanted to develop these ideas in a historical film: "I wanted to show technology at its best, not in a futuristic science fiction world, but by traveling back in time. *Cannon Fodder* was based on Europe during the First World War, and I wanted to go back in time and portray similar themes through an adventure. The words "World's Fair" and "Steam Engine" alone evoke an entire world. They have become landmarks of history. So I chose to set the story in England, a country that has continued to develop pioneering inventions ever since the steam engine."

Taking a break from animation, Otomo's next large-scale project was another live-action film. Fifteen years after the release of *World Apartment Horror*, he began working on the cinematic adaptation of Yuki Urushibara's manga *Mushishi*, thus enabling the director to fulfill one of his fantasies: "I've always been interested in *jidaigeki*[1] and the idea of making one. In Japan, you grow up watching *jidaigeki*. Every filmmaker probably wants to direct one, to be like Akira Kurosawa. But not everyone can be Kurosawa. Plus, I'm not interested in making films that someone else has already made. If I make a film, I want it to be unlike anything else out there. When you stumble across an idea that might allow you to do that—and this was the case with *Mushi-Shi: The Movie*—it really motivates you." Once again, the film's promotion revolved around the fact that it was made "by the creator of *Akira*," and once again, touting the Otomo name wasn't enough to draw in the crowds. Reviews were mixed, praising the feature film's aesthetics while lambasting its storyline, which was hard to follow, especially since Otomo had chosen a non-linear narration that yo-yoed between past and present. And it is indeed a difficult plot to follow unless you're a connoisseur of the manga. In the end, the film struggled to recoup half its budget, despite its success at the Venice and Sundance Film Festivals, both of which preceded its release in Japanese theaters.

Otomo continued on in this retro vein. After his depiction of nineteenth century England and Japan, he became interested in the fire that destroyed 60-70% of the Japanese capital city of Edo (now Tokyo) on March 2, 1657. He thus made the short film *Hi no Yojin* (aka *Combustible*). It was one of four short films in the 2013 anthology *Short Peace* (a name that referred to a manga artist compilation published in 1984). The anthology also featured another short film based on an Otomo story, *Farewell to Weapons*. Like *Kanojo no Omoide*, it had been published in *Young Magazine* just prior to *Akira*. It was directed by the renowned mecha designer Hajime Katoki. Otomo has reflected on this eminently Japanese project: "Its basic theme is fairly typical of old Japanese literature, called kabuki or *joruri*. For example,

---

1. A fictional story most often set during the Edo period (1603 to 1868) or at the beginning of the Meiji era.

the story of Yaoya Oshichi is, more or less, the same as that of *Combustible*. I wanted to take this ancient theme—a theme that was commonplace in Japan 300 years ago—and use existing technology to turn it into an anime."

Jacques Glénat thought that *Akira* had left Otomo drained. And yet, while it is true that Otomo's projects are fewer and far between (and of a lesser scope), he still doesn't seem ready to call it quits. In July 2019, the studio Sunrise announced that he will direct an upcoming animated film entitled *Orbital Era*. The first trailer, which is reminiscent of *2001: A Space Odyssey*, heralds the arrival of a "New Age Movie," and the film's setting is just as mysterious as its release date. But perhaps even more significant was the simultaneous announcement of several new *Akira* projects: first a new 4K remastering of the 1988 cult film, already scheduled for release on April 24, 2020, as well as a new, more enigmatic adaptation, which should be truer to the manga. Its form, however, remains unclear at the time of this publication. Will it be an animated series? Or come in the form of several films? Original video animations, perhaps? No one knows, but Sunrise will once again be the producer, as Otomo gets along with the studio rather well. The manga artist also plans to team up with Kodansha to publish a complete collection of his printed works, with both Japanese and international versions in the works. As for the Hollywood adaptation of *Akira*, which has been in the news since 2002, we'll have to wait a little longer at best. After the struggle to come up with a script, a producer (Leonardo DiCaprio), a director (Taika Waititi), and a 2021 release date, *Thor 4*—also being directed by Waititi—took precedence and again pushed the project back to an undetermined date.

Nonetheless, *Akira*'s legacy lives on, even without Hollywood's blessing. Many directors, of all nationalities, have shamelessly appropriated its themes for their own artistic endeavors. Among the most famous of these directors are the Wachowski sisters: *The Animatrix* anthology film as well as *The Matrix* trilogy definitely bear the mark of *Akira*. So does the nightmarish architecture and anxiety-provoking telekinetic duels of *Dark City* (1998), directed by Alex Proyas. More recently, Josh Trank's excellent film *Chronicle* (2012) appeared to directly mirror Tetsuo's descent into madness through its depiction of a young, tortured protagonist who shares similar telekinetic powers and also ends up going astray. Similarly, the antagonist in Rian Johnson's *Looper* (2012) resembles Akira, with the exception of the criminal syndicate angle. Interestingly, many writers and directors have drawn inspiration from *Akira*'s motif of children with prodigious powers, as was most recently the case in the series *Stranger Things*. Another popular borrowing is the idea of a government conspiracy involving experiments conducted on children with telekinetic powers.

And in many instances, it is not so much the inspiration that shines through, but the frank and direct tribute. *Akira* is now a global pop culture phenomenon, with reference made to it in video clips of Michael Jackson (*Scream*) and Kanye West (*Stronger*) or the fan service extravaganza that is *Ready Player One* (Steven Spielberg, 2018). But by reducing the work of Katsuhiro Otomo to Kaneda's motorcycle, aren't we robbing *Akira* of its subversive nature? Strictly speaking, Otomo is not a revolutionary, but his entire career has been built around harsh societal commentaries and brutal honesty. Unaffected by popular fads and critiques, Otomo expresses himself with all the dignity of a creative type living for his art: "I don't really care what people think of me. A lot of fans complained when I followed *Domu* with *Akira*, and there were more science fiction elements in the former work. Then, I made *Steamboy*, and *Akira* fans wanted to know why. It's always the same. Worrying about other people's opinions, it's counterproductive. I do what I want, and I don't want to fall into a rut. Whatever people think of me and my work, it doesn't matter. I don't think there's any benefit to be had. I'd hate doing the same old thing time and time again."

Otomo has always seen manga as an anti-system tool, a pure and tangible form of expression that can act as an emancipating counterpower, one that is unsubdued by nature. The 2011 disaster that hit Japan on three fronts (earthquake, tsunami, and health catastrophe) rekindled his indignation: "What happened in Fukushima—the nuclear contamination, the displaced people, the inanity of institutions—it brutally plunged me back into the world of *Akira*. Back then, I already knew that this type of disaster would occur. When the economy is the only thing that matters in a society, it's inevitable. The real question is not whether it will happen, but when. There's a reason why my stories feature so many devastating explosions: I'm unfortunately convinced that everything will end this way." Otomo contributed to disaster relief by organizing a major exhibition in Tokyo, called *Genga*, where he put all 2,300 pages of *Akira* and other artworks on display for a two-month period. For a few hundred yen, one could even have a picture of oneself taken on the handlebars of a replica of Kaneda's motorcycle, with the funds going to disaster victims.

The world of manga has changed since *Akira*. As we have previously mentioned, publishers now have much more control over the artistic process, and the market has transformed into one of mass production. Taking into consideration Otomo's non-stories and razor-sharp social satires, not to mention the monumental work that was *Akira*, it seems unlikely that a similar figure will emerge today, especially given contemporary industrial production flows. But there is one thing that Otomo's Japanese and international fans know, and it is confirmed by the fact that he received the Angoulême Grand Prix during the 2015 edition of the world-renowned International Comics Festival (a first for a manga artist): Katsuhiro Otomo is not merely the artist of a single masterpiece, he is the symbol of indomitable creativity, a free spirit who categorically refuses to be labeled. In other words, he is a true artist.

THE IMPACT OF
AKIRA

A MANGA
[R]EVOLUTION

2.1: Creature: Akira
and the A-Bomb Specter

"Manga grew out of the bomb-scorched, barren city, which became a liberating space for postwar Japanese literature. It was especially so for the visual narratives. The ruined black-and-white cityscape became the Original Experience and the Original Picture. It was so clear and transparent that it refused rhetorical elucidation. All the old structures of authority, moral values, and beliefs were destroyed in this space."

Saya Shiraishi[1]

Akira begins with a giant sphere of light over Tokyo. This introduction epitomizes Shiraishi's notion of an original black-and-white picture: one that inevitably depicts an unmitigated disaster and its wake of death and destruction. This image is echoed in the lyrics of *Il y avait une ville*, Claude Nougaro's song about Hiroshima, roughly translated as: "What happened? I don't understand. There was once a city. Now nothing stands." Between 70,000 and 80,000 individuals were instantly killed when *Little Boy* hit Hiroshima. And by the end of 1945, a total of 140,000 people had died from injuries or radiation. This "original experience" served as the inspiration for *Akira*'s prologue: it was said that a catastrophic event, preceding the outbreak of World War III (as opposed to ending World War II), was to occur on December 6, 1982, the day that the series' first chapter was to be published in *Weekly Young Magazine*...

We then flash-forward thirty-eight years, a period that corresponds to the time between the dropping of the atomic bombs on Japan and the publication of *Akira*. Otomo has never explicitly referred to the obvious juxtaposition between his work and the scars inflicted by the events of August 1945; he really didn't need to, since as Saya Shiraishi has said, original experience rules out the need for "rational explanations." The impressive number of fictional Japanese narratives with the traumatic outcome of WWII as their backdrop, or even just as a simple subtext, bears witness to the importance of symbols, their power, and even their necessity: the Japanese people needed to tell their story. And yet, symbols do not have

1. Peter J. Katzenstein and Takashi Shiraishi. *Network Power: Japan and Asia*. Cornell University Press, 1997.

the virtue of being instructive, let alone explicit. They go above and beyond such concerns: symbols suggest and embody ideas better than words ever could. They do not represent an intellectual or political position, but speak directly to the mind and heart, bypassing reason at times.

Art has always been the expression of a feeling that is too subtle to be expressed in mere words. In the aftermath of the war, an entire body of literature (referred to as *genbaku bunkagu*) developed around the concrete memory of the atomic bomb, but the forms taken by this artistic expression soon surpassed simple war stories and survivor testimonies. The terror associated with the bomb, indiscriminate destruction, and the idea of an "end" as violent as it is inevitable continues to be a fertile breeding ground for many authors, visual artists, musicians, playwrights, and directors.

And amongst the writers, there were, of course, the first manga artists. The "God of Manga," Osamu Tezuka, and many artists of his generation had a number of war stories to tell. Born in the 1920s, they became direct witnesses to–and sometimes unwilling proponents of–Japan's military escalation during the 1930s. They also saw its consequences: the ruin of a country, the downfall of a system, and hundreds of thousands of deaths. Tezuka, whose work and anti-war activism we will soon discuss, confided in his autobiographical manga *Kami no toride* (aka *The Paper Fortress*) that he himself was confronted with the death and chaos of the American bombings in 1944, while he stood watch at the top of a tower overlooking the arms factory where he worked:[2] "As the air raid warning siren began, I saw that as usual, a formation of US bombers was heading toward us along the Yodogawa River. As soon as I thought 'here they come,' incendiary bombs showered down on us, making a loud noise like a heavy rain. Bombs streamed down onto the factory, one after another. Just when I thought that this would be the end of my life, exposed on the top of the watchtower, a bomb hit the roof directly below me, only six and a half feet away. Later I heard that this bomb killed all the people who had rushed into the air raid shelter underneath this building. I tumbled down the watchtower, screaming as if I had gone mad. All around me, the ground was a sea of fire [...], and houses in every direction were burning with leaping flames making a rumbling sound. Then rain with black soot came down. I walked to the top of the riverbank of the Yodogawa. From there, I saw many big craters hollowed by bombs, where numerous objects resembling human bodies were lying on top of one another. The bodies were so fractured that they did not look like human beings."[3]

---

2. Incidentally, this task had been assigned to him as a punishment, since he spent much of his time drawing rather than working.
3. Yuki Tanaka. "War and Peace in the Art of Tezuka Osamu: The Humanism of his Epic Manga." *The Asia Pacific Journal*, 38-1-10, 20 Sept. 2010.

Tezuka wasn't the only one to share his traumatic experience. Shigeru Mizuki, the author of *GeGeGe no Kitaro* (aka *Kitaro of the Graveyard*, 1959) served in the Imperial Army in 1942. He became ill after contracting malaria, saw his comrades die in battle, and lost his right arm during an Allied bombardment. This did not end his career, however: he learned to draw with his left hand and became one of the greatest anti-war proponents in the manga world. And then there is Keiji Nakazawa's highly successful cult work, *Hadashi no Gen* (aka *Barefoot Gen*, 1973), which recounted the horror of Hiroshima. Hideshi Hino's more recent *Jigokuhen* (aka *Panorama of Hell*, 1984) is written from a somewhat different perspective: his semi-autobiographical manga traces his family's flight from Manchuria at the end of the war. The work, which is definitely not to everyone's taste, creates considerable unease since it mixes anecdotes and sordid exaggerations, without anyone really knowing which stories are true and which are fiction. And then there is Tetsuya Chiba, who illustrated the 1968 manga boxing series *Ashita no Joe* (a tribute to the left-wing youth of the late 1960s). He could also relate to the difficulties of leaving China and returning to Japan once the war had ended, as it was a personal experience that he found quite painful.

Like many of his colleagues, including those mentioned above, Tezuka did not emerge from this traumatic episode unscathed. His work is a direct result of it, an exorcism with an activist feel that is part of a profoundly anti-war discourse. It isn't hard to see its distant echo, so much like the European slogan "never again." Seven years later, after having seen hell and cheated death, Tezuka published *Tetsuwan Atomu*, known in the West as *Astro Boy*. A science fiction reimagining of *Pinocchio*—Tezuka has never denied the fact that he was largely inspired by Disney throughout his career—Atomu eventually became one of the most important characters of Japanese pop culture (and certainly the most famous in the history of manga).[4] The "original experience" was echoed in his name, Atomu, which unfortunately did not escape censorship when it was exported to the West. The subject of the atomic bomb was still sensitive for the Americans, whose television channels did not enjoy the same degree of freedom as those in Japan. Like the title of his very first adventure (and Tezuka himself), Atomu is an ambassador for peace.[5] His escapades cannot be reduced to a simplistic Manichean struggle between good and evil. Instead, they address more complex problems and repeatedly warn us of the risks

---

4. *Tetsuwan Atomu* was the first thirty-minute weekly anime broadcast on Japanese television.
5. Atomu appeared for the first time in *Atomu Taishi* (*Ambassador Atom*), a moderately successful serialized manga. Despite the name of the title, he was not the main character. Atomu did not become a superstar until he was featured in the *Tetsuwan Atomu* series (1952-1968).

of escalation. Although the series is not devoid of action, Atomu finds solutions to avert misfortune rather than fighting villains. For example, to ensure that robots and humans live harmoniously in his futuristic world, Atomu protects the first robot preparing to vote, then serves as a bodyguard to the first robot president, and subsequently defuses a conflict between humans and extraterrestrials fighting over natural resources. *Tetsuwan Atomu* reflects many problematic issues of post-war Japan: the fate of orphans (Atomu was abandoned by his creator), the dangers of misapplied science, xenophobia, military escalation, etc. These themes are not unique to *Tetsuwan Atomu*: they are found in all of Tezuka's work. The manga artist had already written an uncompromising critique of the nascent power struggle between the United States and the Soviet Union before his success with Atomu. This came in the form of the 1951 *Kitarubeki Sekai* (aka *Next World*, Taifu Comics), a two-volume manga featuring a Japanese professor named Dr. Yamadano, who warns the nations of the world about the dangers of atomic testing after fallout has caused terrible mutations to the flora and fauna of a mysterious island. His warnings are quickly drowned out by the cartoon-like rants of war-mongering officials in Star (the USA) and Uran (the USSR), who foolishly turn the issue into a political contest instead of seeing it from a humanist perspective.[6] The scene showing Yamadano shouting at an assembly of career politicians looks a lot like Katsuhiro Otomo's Colonel Shikishima in *Akira*, when he warns the political elite about the danger of Akira and the imminence of his return. Like many young boys of his generation, Otomo was indeed an avid reader of the "god" Tezuka (ATOM would be the name of his super-computer in *Fireball*). *Kitarubeki Sekai*'s message was crystal clear and best expressed by Dr. Yamadano: "We don't have time to talk about draft amendments anymore! I'm here to try to put a definitive stop to the use of atomic weapons!"

Another witness to the horror of the war and its repercussions was Keiji Nakazawa, whose previously mentioned work *Barefoot Gen* made him famous. Compared to Osamu Tezuka, Nakazawa was even more of a victim of the "original experience" as he was only about a half mile away from the epicenter of the bomb blast that razed his hometown of Hiroshima on August 9, 1945, when he was only six years old. His sister, father, and brother perished in the disaster, and the shock forced his mother, eight months pregnant, to give birth alone by the side of the road. The baby died four months later. Nakazawa said that he himself had to find the bones of

---

6. Tezuka filled up an entire large manga panel showing all the representatives bickering like children on a playground.

his family members in the rubble. The manga artist could easily confuse *Barefoot Gen*'s story with his own personal one: the infernal landscape described by Tezuka overlaps with the horror Nakazawa bore witness to in his work and in the interviews he was able to give during his lifetime (he died of lung cancer in Hiroshima in 2012, at the age of seventy-three). His mother passed away in 1966, and her cremation profoundly shocked Nakazawa: her bones, eaten away by radiation, did not leave a single ash. This was just one more traumatic event that further strengthened his commitment to activism. And indeed, the name "Gen" was not chosen at random. Nakazawa pointed out that "the young protagonist's name, has several meanings in Japanese. It can mean the 'root' or 'origin' of something, but also 'elemental' in the sense of an atomic element, as well as a 'source' of vitality and happiness. I envisioned Gen barefoot, standing firmly atop the burnt-out rubble of Hiroshima, raising his voice against war and nuclear weapons." The idea of an origin, of a fertile starting point, is suggested at length in *Akira*, especially in the manga version where the power of the boy is compared to the Big Bang, to the creation of a new universe. *Barefoot Gen* concludes with the growth of a new wheat crop.

The catastrophic bomb is rarely evoked without a profound message of hope, a "recovery" after the worst of ordeals. It was certainly this ability to look forward that allowed the Japanese to recover after 1945 and produce what history would later call the "Japanese miracle." This need for hope is evident in post-war fiction, whether realistic or allegorical. Literature, manga, and cinema have reappropriated the chaos of war to reconstruct an emancipatory narrative, and they continue to do so today. And even when the tragedy is total, we often find the idea of an afterlife, of rest for the souls who have been tried and tested and are now ready to embark on a journey of a different kind. In *Hotaru no Haka* (aka *Grave of the Fireflies*, 1988), by Isao Takahata,[7] the two young protagonists, Seita and his sister Setsuko, die of malnutrition a few months after losing their mother in a bombing raid on their town of Kobe. The film recounts their slow agony, punctuating it with happy moments, such as when Seita finds a box of sweets for Setsuko (which he will eventually use for his sister's ashes, since she precedes him in death). Although they both die, their spirits find peace: the last scene shows them together, watching a modern Kobe basking in the lights of its recovery.

Ishiro Honda's *Godzilla* (1954) was the first large-scale example of a reinterpretation of history, a digestion of the events that occurred at

---

7. An adaptation of Akiyuki Nosaka's semi-autobiographical short story, *Grave of the Fireflies*.

the end of the war and which would, ultimately, enable Japan to emerge stronger. Before becoming a creature who resembles the friendly reptile in *Denver, the Last Dinosaur*, Godzilla symbolized American antagonism and the dangers of weapons of mass destruction. (The monster was originally an ancient sea creature, transformed and finally awakened by the US military's hydrogen bomb tests). But the Japan shown in the film is not a passive victim helplessly watching events unfold in Hiroshima and Nagasaki. The country decides to take matters into its own hands and find a way to defeat Godzilla. While death and material damages accumulate, a scientist, Serizawa, manages to use his research on the atom to develop a weapon capable of asphyxiating Godzilla. He ends up a sacrificial hero, ultimately activating the device himself in the Tokyo Bay area. Before dying, he destroys all his notes and formulas, lest they fall into the wrong hands. The outcome is telling: a victorious Japan transcends the mourning of August 1945 by appropriating the science that was at the origin of its suffering.

The atom, the bomb, the radiation: the Japanese never truly forgot these sorrows after the defeat. Quite the opposite, since the film was released only a few months after the *Lucky Dragon* affair, which had inflamed Japanese public debate and greatly influenced the creation of *Godzilla*. The *Lucky Dragon No. 5 (Daigo Fukuryu Maru)* was a tuna boat caught in the radioactive fallout from the *Castle Bravo* hydrogen bomb test on Bikini Atoll in the Marshall Islands on March 1, 1954. Much more powerful than expected, the bomb's explosion largely exceeded the predictions of the American army, which had defined a danger zone that was too small, even though the Japanese sailors had respected it. Falling ill quickly, they debarked in the town of Yaizu for treatment two weeks later. All were suffering from the symptoms of acute radiation, and their radio operator died from it six months later. The matter became a burning issue for the US military when it was revealed that the real danger zone had been crossed by about 100 ships and that, as a result, contaminated goods had already started to circulate in Japanese markets.[8] Over the years, the fear of radiation—present in many of Ishiro Honda's films, including *The H-Man* (1958) and *Matango* (1963)—transformed into worries about a bacteriological crisis. This dread is depicted in Masaya Hokazono's manga *Emerging* (2004). Following the patterns of many Japanese-style apocalyptic fictional works, this manga is about a strange virus that leads to a monster epidemic in Tokyo: politicians are caricatures of corrupt rich people, the origin of the virus is never known (a sudden, perhaps deliberate, assault of nature is

---

8. In a desperate attempt to defuse the controversy, the head of the US Atomic Energy Commission alleged that the *Daigo Fukuryu Maru* had been sent to spy on the tests.

suspected), and the United States intervenes in one way or another. Here, the virus is sent to Uncle Sam's country for analysis, "dispossessing" the Japanese of the keys to their destiny. Just as in Sakyo Komatsu's *Nihon Chinbotsu* (aka *Japan Sinks*, 1973), it is the end of Japan (and not the end of the world) that is the story's focus. The relationship between nations is an integral part of disaster management, and *Akira* is no stranger to this idea: at the end of the manga, international aid is refused, and the new "Great Empire of Akira" prefers self-determination rather than subordination, an echo of the American occupation at the end of WWII.

But let's return to *Godzilla* and other latex monsters. Known for his work as a monster designer for the Ultra Series (*Ultraman Q, Ultraman*, and *Ultra Seven*) in the late sixties, Toru Narita was part of the *Godzilla* production's *tokusatsu* (special effects) team. Many of his sculpted creatures have monstrous features, exaggerated by the effects of radiation. In his 1966 work entitled *Tokusatsu to Kaiju* (aka *Special Effects and Giant Monsters*), he explained that he himself had been a victim of the American raids during the war, and that he believed his life's great mission was to "describe the moment when *Little Boy*[9] exploded over Hiroshima." *Spectreman*,[10] a *tokusatsu* television drama that came out a few years later, moved from radiation to the similarly problematic issue of pollution, as Tokyo had then become the most polluted city in the world. The antagonist, Dr. Gori (a kind of alien ape-man), is looking for a planet to colonize and sets his sights on Earth. Appalled by the fact that the ecosystem is being threatened by human activities, he decides to get rid of this annoying species by turning its own transgressions against it. He uses the pollution to create hideous monsters that Spectreman, an alien from another planet, must defeat if he is to save humanity. Whether it's radiation or pollution, the emphasis is always on the activity of humankind, our ethical choices and our relationship with the environment.

The seventies transported this thematic nebula, addressing war and its consequences, to the vaster backdrop of space. In 1974, Japanese television first broadcast what would become one of the pillars of Japanese space opera: *Uchu Senkan Yamato*, better known in the West as *Space Battleship Yamato*. Directed by Leiji Matsumoto, the future creator of *Space Pirate Captain Harlock* and *Galaxy Express 999*, the twenty-six episode series plunges the spectator into an apocalyptic future. The ecosystem of the Earth, whose surface has become uninhabitable following the radioactive bombardments of an extraterrestrial race, appears doomed. Humanity,

9. The codename of the bomb dropped on Hiroshima. The one that hit Nagasaki was called *Fat Man*.
10. *Spectreman* arrived in North America in the late seventies and in France in the early eighties.

which had taken refuge in immense underground cities, is gradually being affected by the radioactivity permeating the soil, leaving it with little hope of survival. During a simple routine mission to Mars, the protagonist, Susumu Kodai, discovers a message in the wreckage of a crashed spaceship. It is from the distant planet Iscandar, whose queen claims to possess a device capable of decontaminating the environment and thus saving humanity. Because Iscandar is thousands of light-years away from Earth, the message also contains blueprints for a revolutionary engine that would allow travel beyond the solar system, something humankind had never been able to do before. The engine is finally installed in an old WWII vessel, the *Yamato*, transforming the wreck into a state-of-the-art battleship, the last hope of humanity.

The tale is one of reappropriation and transcendence. The symbolic power of *Space Battleship Yamato*'s scenario has few equivalents, and the levels of reading are multiple. Is it an ecological fable? An ode to hope, however distant? A reconciliation with the past? Leiji Matsumoto's work is a bit of all of these. It is important to note that the *Yamato* was a real battleship and that she had the kind of tragic history that the Japanese are particularly fond of. The pride of Japan's naval forces during WWII, the *Yamato* was a veritable floating fortress, capable of engaging a large number of enemies at the same time. Although it wasn't used extensively during the war, the prestige associated with this marvel of military engineering still resonates in the hearts of the Japanese, seventy-five years after its destruction. The *Yamato*'s last mission (Operation Ten-Go) has that poetic beauty characteristic of Japanese tragedies, since the battleship was sent as a last-ditch effort to defend Okinawa, which had been invaded by the Allied forces. With insufficient fuel for the return journey—not to mention clear evidence that the Allies had the upper hand—the officers of the *Yamato* knew they were leaving on a one-way mission, the end of which was preordained. But the Japanese never gave up, and the heroism of the officers killed in action on April 7, 1945 still serves as a reminder of their resolve in the face of adversity, of the Japanese fighting spirit that we will further examine in subsequent chapters. Released in 2005, the film *Yamato* (aka *Otoko-tachi no Yamato*, literally *The Men's Yamato*) was very well received in Japanese cinemas, even if, as with James Cameron's *Titanic* (1997), everyone knew that in the end, the ship would sink. For the record, one of Matsumoto's main inspirations for the making of *Space Battleship Yamato* was Shigeru Komatsuzaki's paintings, especially those depicting naval battles, including, of course, one portraying the battleship *Yamato*.

Resurrected via Iscandar's technology, the *Yamato* also goes on a last-chance mission in Leiji Matsumoto's series. Seeing as the radiation pollution is destroying the Earth's ecosystem, the vessel must retrieve the decontamination device and return to Earth within a one-year deadline. But the series thumbs its nose at history since, this time, the battleship makes it back to its port. The ship's captain (Juzo Okita), whose health continues to decline throughout the voyage, peacefully dies right before arrival, much like Moses catching a glimpse of the Promised Land. The captain of the historic *Yamato*, the one who piloted the ship during Operation Ten-Go, makes an appearance in the 1977 feature-length animated film based on the series. He is voiced by the same actor (Goro Naya) who did the voice-over for Captain Okita. In any event, before Okita dies in the series, he entrusts the *Yamato* to the protagonist Susumu, whose name means "to advance, to move forward."

Chock-full of symbolism, the *Space Battleship Yamato* series is hardly a rarity in Japanese fiction. On the contrary, it's a textbook example. Artists like Leiji Matsumoto have continuously reinvented new ways of evoking history, imbuing their work with a humanist message that transcends national, ideological, and spiritual boundaries.

A few years after *Space Battleship Yamato*, the series *Mobile Suit Gundam* (1979) presented similar themes by incorporating a more political dimension into its interstellar conflicts. And yet, once again, the series cannot be reduced to a simplistic Manichean struggle between good and evil. Only actions, and not people, are considered bad (i.e. disastrous). One of the major catastrophes of the "One Year War" that serves as a background to the series is thus: the Principality of Zeon, which wants to gain its independence from the Earth Federation, is guilty of the hijacking and crashing of a space colony on Earth, causing billions of deaths and the consequent signing of an "Antarctic Treaty" that bans the future use of weapons of mass destruction, as well as the use of colonies as cannonballs. The creator and director of *Mobile Suit Gundam*, Yoshiyuki Tomino (who had previously worked with Tezuka on *Astro Boy*), came out with another large-scale space opera with similar beginnings, a year later: *Densetsu Kyojin Ideon* (aka *Space Runaway Ideon*). But it was the series' ending and ultimately the film *Space Runaway Ideon: Be Invoked* that fleshed out the story and really hit home, since all of the protagonists, humans and aliens alike, both "good guys" and "bad," die in an extremely violent battle, before the few remaining survivors are finally killed by a blast that wipes out much of the universe. The last scene shows the naked souls of the protagonists, leaving for a new world, full of hope. The ruthless brutality of the film's last minutes (with a child's decapitation being graphically depicted) is forgotten. Friends and lovers are reunited, grudges fade away, and the viewer is almost be tempted to think "all's well that ends well." In the face of catastrophe, only eternal optimism remains, just as in *Grave of the Fireflies*. And indeed, Tomino is not one to shy away from violence.

In *Seisenshi Danbain* (aka *Aura Battler Dunbine*, 1983), nearly the entire cast perishes in the final battle, sometimes quite expeditiously, leaving Cham, the little fairy accompanying the protagonist, as the sole survivor. Tomino's proclivity to wipe out all his characters in a great final battle earned him the nickname "Kill 'Em All Tomino"...

The notion of a major disaster that destroys Japan and its helpless inhabitants has never been limited to the atomic bomb. And because progress and ethics are paramount when dealing with science and its use, the question of the environment rears its head. As we have previously seen, the problem of pollution and the impact of technological progress on nature has increasingly entered into public debate since the 1970s. The menace of an angry, resentful planet responding to the destruction of its ecosystem by directly or indirectly attacking humanity has become a common fictional narrative. Hayao Miyazaki is a pioneer, even a prophet, of this new "eco-consciousness." His work is a hymn to nature in all its ambivalence: she is sometimes a nurturing mother and sometimes an ogress. The living things that populate the Earth are neither our friends nor our enemies. It is up to us to determine the relationship we will have with them and our environment. This ambivalence is found in Shintoism, the native religion of Japan, which professes that the Japanese archipelago is populated by kamis, spirits present in everything that exists. As opposed to monotheistic religions with a benevolent God and an evil rival (Satan), Japanese kamis do not fit into Manichean logic: they are kind when treated well and hostile when disrespected. And not only is this true of nature in Miyazaki's work, it is the scientific proposition of post-war fiction, i.e. that humankind can only thrive if natural energies are used wisely. Conversely, a malevolent use of science by individuals corrupted by pride can only lead to chaos and dual destruction: that of humankind and of nature. Miyazaki has addressed these questions at length in his feature films. The anti-war message in his work is similar to that of his peers, Tezuka, Mizuki, and Takahata included. At the age of twenty-eight, fifteen years before his first big hit, *Kaze no tani no Naushika* (aka *Nausicaa of the Valley of the Wind*), Miyazaki penned a 1969 manga entitled *Sabaku no tami* (aka *People of the Desert*), considered by some to be the spiritual ancestor of *Nausicaa*. It is one of the animation master's rare mangas, along with *Nausicaa*! It has a rather odd format, with the story divided into twenty-six chapters, each comprised of two pages. Looking almost like a storyboard, the work features rough drawings, and speech bubbles are often absent, with the spotty narration appearing as small blocks of text next to the panels. But that was all Miyazaki needed to tell a powerful, tragic, and no-frills tale. *Sabaku no tami* takes place in a fictional ancient China and relates the adventures of young Tem, an orphaned boy who tries to evade a barbarian tribe that destroys, plunders, and enslaves all those who have the misfortune of crossing its path. While the manga boldly depicts the human soul at its most repulsive, it also features noble and courageous spirits, individuals who do not hesitate to sacrifice themselves for others. Miyazaki's work is violent in its details as well as in its subject matter, and despite its rudimentary look, it manages to cut the reader to the quick, with a conclusion that is as dramatic as it is open-ended. The last chapter concludes with the barbarians' defeat, but Tem has lost all his comrades in the course of his adventure, including the one he had fallen in love with (she contracts the plague and dies). The end is brutal, and peace—as Tem declares in the last frame—is far from being reached. But isn't this Miyazaki expressing himself through his young hero, thus concluding his pessimistic fable whose historical echoes seem obvious?

The avoidance of war is the leitmotif of the protagonists in both *Nausicaa* and *Mononoke Hime* (aka *Princess Mononoke*, 1997). Despite the twelve-year interval between their release dates, the subject of both works is essentially the same: the unstable equilibrium between humankind and nature. Like Tezuka's Atomu, the titular character in the former work, Nausicaa, acts as a mediator, an ambassador for peace on the eve of an international conflict. The world in which she lives is still recovering from a dreadful war, known as the Seven Days of Fire. In their madness, humankind opened a Pandora's box by assembling giant god warriors, weapons whose colossal power had terrible consequences for the environment. From the ashes of the war grew the Toxic Jungle. It gradually gained ground and now threatens the surviving populations (an idea that overlaps with the plot of *Space Battleship Yamato*). In the film, the Tolmekian Empire gets its hands on the embryo of a god warrior, which it intends to use to destroy both the Toxic Jungle and the ohm, giant insects perceived as a threat to the human race. Nausicaa does not see nature as a danger and values all creatures. During her adventures, she discovers that the Toxic Jungle functions as the planet's immune system. The Earth has created this forest to decontaminate its soil and purify its waters. The impatient Tolmekian Empire makes no attempt to understand the workings of nature. The Toxic Forest is the result of humankind's arrogance, the same arrogance that pushes the Tolmekians to mature the god warrior and thus trigger a new catastrophe (and here, we are reminded of the unhealthy fascination of *Akira*'s scientists, who do not learn from the lessons of history). Kurotawa, a Tolmekian general, fantasizes about the weapon's capabilities and begins to openly express his admiration for it: "I swear, the more I gaze at you, the more attractive you get. I can't wait to see you at work. You're awaking long-forgotten ambitions in me. [...] The likes of you should have slept underground until the end of time!" Pejite, an enemy nation of the

Tolmekian Empire, then captures a wounded baby ohm and uses it as bait to attract a gigantic swarm of adult ohms, thus driving the insects toward the Tolmekian imperial guard. The latter uses the god warrior to fire at the giant insects, killing some of them in the process. The resulting explosion resembles an atomic mushroom cloud. The image's symbolic power is underscored by two remarks. Kurotawa says, "This is the weapon that destroyed the world" and old Oh-Baba responds, "If people become slaves to such a powerful weapon, they cannot live in harmony with the Earth." Incidentally, the scene with the god-warrior firing on the ohms was animated by a young Hideaki Anno, the future creator of *Neon Genesis Evangelion*, a popular series depicting the artist's own apocalyptic vision and humankind's place in the world. But back to our story. The hostilities continue until Nausicaa attempts a desperate maneuver: she uses her body to block the swarm of ohms, who trample her before slowing down and finally coming to a halt. Because she has proven herself capable of self-sacrifice, the insects cure (or rather resuscitate) her, and the conflict comes to an end.

Princess Mononoke has much in common with Nausicaa, both in terms of its themes and its structure. This time, the emissary is a young man named Ashitaka, whose quest will lead him into multiple conflicts, with humans opposed to other humans, humans opposed to nature, and nature opposed to itself. And, once again, the story is not about good versus evil: it is about ignorance. The beasts, spirits, and gods all have numerous flaws, but it is hate that is identified as the source of all evils. Ashitaka's mantra is that hatred only leads to more hatred. Most of the characters he meets, whether human or animal, try to justify their animosity by posing as victims. But, because they do not have an open mind, they only perpetuate the cycle. Nago, the giant boar that struck Ashitaka's arm with a deadly curse, only became a demon because he surrendered to his hatred after being wounded by hunters. The latter have deforested the area around their village to produce iron, thus enraging the forest creatures. The animals thus attack the humans, who defend themselves by producing more iron. Each side is locked in their perpetual hatred, with their own prejudices. Even the fierce Princess Mononoke herself, known as San, despises humans (as she was raised by wolves). Ashitaka is also far from perfect: his idealism borders on naivety when he accuses Lady Eboshi, the charismatic manager of the forge that makes the feared weapons, of "sowing only destruction and hatred." Eboshi does seek to expand her territory, but not out of ego. She takes in the wretched ex-prostitutes and marginalized lepers, enabling them to work with dignity. This allows them to form a community that is united in adversity, where there is no judgment. And yet, such arguments do not convince Ashitaka, who becomes overwhelmed with anger. Indeed, his cursed arm convulses whenever dark thoughts enter his mind. This short scene highlights all the complexity of a situation that indolent minds perceive in a binary way: there is not necessarily a "good" side and a "bad" side. Mutual understanding is required, and the aim of any solution should be to cause the least amount of harm (at worst) or bring about peace (at best).

This message overlaps with the notion of nature's ambivalence, for nature is both bountiful and dangerous. Miyazaki is no tree-hugging, joint-smoking hippie. Nature gives life, but its forces can also take it, like the Great Forest Spirit (the deer-like god in the second half of the film). He is an avatar of nature, with a rather human-looking face. Could this be a mirror-like symbol of our dependence on the environment (or perhaps our impact on it)? In any event, he is cruelly decapitated by Eboshi, who intends to give his head to the emperor. And yet, the Forest Spirit doesn't just die. Instead, he is transformed into a gigantic, vaguely anthropomorphic, gelatinous mass, whose mere touch instantly kills all forms of life. The creature's shape, texture, and uncontrolled spasms are reminiscent of Tetsuo's ego death and subsequent transformation at the end of *Akira*: in both cases, an astonishing, transcendental power emerges once the guiding force of the ego is shed. The Forest Spirit is now the perfect embodiment of death: like the Grim Reaper, he does not discriminate. Ashitaka and San are only able to appease him—and thus stop the nightmare—by returning his head to him. The Forest Spirit finally disappears, but his powers heal Ashitaka and cause the desolate mountainside to bloom again. As for Eboshi, she vows to be more sensitive to the fate of the animals. Her prideful nature literally costs her an arm (but not a leg) in the tale, whereas Ashitaka's dedicated efforts earn him the use of his.

The fire of the god warriors, the catapulting of the space colonies, and each mushroom cloud reference the same nightmare. This portrayal of large-scale annihilation, whether on the screen or in the pages of a manga, served as a kind of Japanese group therapy following the shared trauma. But, over time, it also became a part of pop culture. This is perhaps best expressed in the animated short film produced for the 1983 Daicon IV[11] Nihon SF Taikai convention, one of the world's oldest science fiction conventions (its first edition was held in 1962). The opening animation is an important part of anime history, a smorgasbord of sci-fi references

11. Each convention was named after its venue. In the case of Daicon, the first kanji character of Osaka (大阪市), where it was held, can be pronounced "dai." The "con" is the first syllable of convention, and it was the fourth convention to be held in Osaka, hence the 4.

and a festive *battle royale*, chock full of Eastern and Western references from *Gundam* to *Star Wars*. The opening short was directed and produced by a dozen or so upcoming animators, including Hideaki Anno, Takami Akai, and Yoshiyuki Sadamoto from the Daicon Film studio. Barely in their twenties, these young men changed the studio's name to Gainax two years later and then enjoyed such smashing successes as *Gunbuster* (1988), *Fushigi no umi no Nadia* (*Nadia: the Secret of Blue Water*, 1990), and *Neon Genesis Evangelion* (1995), all of which were directed by Anno.

The short was finished just in the nick of time, i.e. the morning of the convention's opening! It superbly highlighted a remark about art in a videocassette advertisement featuring Taro Okamoto (1911-1996), who famously said: "Art is an explosion!" After a flashback recalling the events of *Daicon III* (created for the 1981 edition by Anno, Akai, and their colleague Hiroyuki Yamaga), the five-minute-long *Daicon IV* short managed to embody the idea of fan service by squeezing in dozens of popular sci-fi references, both Japanese and Western: the heroine, wearing a sexy bunny costume (the one made famous by *Playboy*) kills monsters and giant robots with a simple kick, engages in a lightsaber duel with Darth Vader, surfs through the sky on the Stormbringer sword, and crosses the Macross fortress, a Klingon ship, and the *Space Battleship Yamato*, before they all crash into each other like bumper cars... Then, what looks like an atomic bomb explodes in the middle of a deserted city, with the detonation generating billions of cherry blossom petals and causing the mountains to rise. The heroine's spaceship, which she had created by watering a large black radish (a daikon, for the pun based on the name of the convention), then fires a beam of light that regenerates the planet. This is followed by a final group photo and a shot of the Earth from space.

But *Daicon IV* isn't just a tribute to pop culture. And it's not just a silly attempt to make fans respond to its many cameos. *Daicon IV* is the literal and figurative "explosion" of the visceral need to produce, to express oneself, to communicate. It is a heartfelt cry that ignored copyrights by appropriating the Playboy bunny costume and using the Electric Light Orchestra's *Twilight* as a soundtrack (which compromises its distribution in stores, despite the unofficial release of a LaserDisc coupled with an art book that is now quite popular with collectors). Art is an explosion, the irrepressible and necessary emergence of powerful emotions, which can take forms as varied as the range of characters, vessels, critters, and worlds briefly portrayed in *Daicon IV*. In the end, it is creative energy that resuscitates the devastated, arid land, simply through the power of imagination.

And Anno appears to be fascinated by the bewitching and terrifying iconography of the atomic bomb. As we have previously mentioned, he worked on the scene where the god warrior fires on the ohms in *Nausicaa* but, in addition to *Daicon IV*, we have him to thank for animating several similar scenes in Episode 27 of *Chojiku Yosai Macross* (*Super Dimension Fortress Macross*), which aired in 1983, the same year that *Daicon IV* was held. The scenes of destruction during the great space battle are extremely detailed: the difference in temperature between the hot and cold air changes the direction of the wind, the disintegration of wooden structures differs from that of metallic ones, etc. Everything happens very quickly, but the realism is striking. Anno later explained that he spent a good deal of time studying nuclear test films in order to make these short sequences.

No matter how you look at it, Japan has always had a complicated relationship with its history. Its involvement in World War II and the Pacific Wars is no exception, as it brings up issues of identity, relationship to the state, responsibility, and acceptance of failure. Speaking about the brutality of war, Osamu Tezuka himself stated: "We must not turn away from the reality, saying that it has nothing to do with us and therefore ignoring it. If we really want world peace, this is where we have to start."[12] In the aftermath of the war, the American occupation tightened the screws on censorship and confiscated all images of Hiroshima and Nagasaki after the bombings (before returning them in the 1960s). Martial arts manga and historical adventures were also banned until the Americans left the archipelago in 1952. Japan was thus unable to lick its wounds while they were still raw. It was only able to do so after years of profound transformation. This made it seem like the revisiting of history wasn't a priority, like it was too far in the distant past. The country had already turned its eyes to the future, and what a future it would be! Japan was now "demilitarized," as agreed in Article 9 of its new constitution, which made it "forever renounce war as a sovereign right of the nation" (an article whose interpretation has changed over years, in keeping with American needs) while remaining under the diplomatic wing of Uncle Sam for many long years. Noi Sawaragi, an art critic and professor at Tama University, said that Japan lost its sense of history in the years after the war because "the positive visions of 'peace' and 'rapid economic growth' upheld in Japan since 1945 were nothing but artificial constructs, preserved under the guardianship of the US as head of the Western bloc, with a blind eye turned to the bloody proxy wars being waged in Korea and Vietnam. Throughout the 1960s, the New Left repeatedly challenged the power of the state, mobilizing young people and students who understood that such 'peace' was a fabrication preserved through the conflicts of the Cold War. But

12. Osamu Tezuka. *War: Lambs of Sacrifice*. Tezuka Productions.

THE IMPACT OF AKIRA: A MANGA [R]EVOLUTION

their decisive defeat in the struggle against the renewal of the US-Japan Security Treaty in 1970 forced the New Left into irrelevance [see next chapter].[13] With all resistance toward the fiction of peace now silenced, the Japanese people rapidly withdrew into an ahistorical capsule, losing sight of their own history and thus the sense of the wider world in which their past had unfolded. This ahistorical 'withdrawal' (jihei) eventually led to what may be called an 'imaginary reality': the 'bubble economy' caused by the speculative frenzy of land buying in the 1980s."[14] Interestingly, this 'withdrawal' took a blow after the death of Emperor Hirohito in 1989, an event that prompted the Japanese to question the role and responsibility of their sovereign in the Pacific defeat, and thus to re-examine what was arguably the worst episode in their history. This was the epilogue to the Japanese 'economic miracle,' and the 1990s would mark the end of the dream by bursting the bubble and questioning the post-war narrative and the 'withdrawal' explained by Sawaragi.

Artists like Tezuka, Mizuki, and Nakazawa were there to evoke these past wounds though autobiographical works (or works charged with symbolic energy). *Akira* also espoused this idea of a buried transgression, of a shameful past whose discovery could change the face of the world. It did so by hiding its titular little boy six feet underground, imprisoned behind many sealed doors, military protocols, armed guards and, in the end, inside a coffin plunged into absolute zero where all organic life is incapable of surviving. In the manga version, there are two ways to enter these underground labyrinths: the first entrance is next to the Olympic Stadium under construction, and the other is right in the middle of the crater where Akira woke up thirty years earlier. Katsuhiro Otomo thus makes the connection between the pride of the post-war period, symbolized by the 1964 Tokyo Olympic Games, and ground zero of the atomic disaster, which are inseparable. These Games served as a showcase for post-war Japan, a way for the country to show off its valiant and determined population and international status despite the changing world and the 1945 defeat. The difference between the two passages leading to Akira's room is that the entrance to the military base is heavily secured, while the entrance to the crater, which is closed to the public, acts as an 'emergency exit', a secret, hidden corridor that Tetsuo takes after releasing Akira.

In this exhumation of History, Tetsuo's actions are fated: he does not need to ask others how to find his prey. Because he is able to read thoughts, he ventures effortlessly into the minds of the gatekeepers, the secret keepers

---

13. Author's Note.
14. Noi Sawaragi. "On The Battlefield of 'Superflat,' Subculture and Art In Postwar Japan." Excerpt from *Little Boy: The Arts of Japan's Exploding Subculture*, Yale University Press, 2005.

who have never paid the price for their past actions. The authorities have buried Akira: they have camouflaged the reality of the catastrophe that razed Tokyo to the ground until a resurrected, modernized but breathless society violently expels this relic of the past, brought to the surface by a new miscalculation named Tetsuo. The teenager embodies past mistakes. He is the logical consequence of humankind's madness, because as Albert Einstein once said: "The definition of insanity is doing the same thing over and over again and expecting a different result."

Renewal always comes in the form of youth, and this is all the more true in Japanese manga and animation. According to Hayao Miyazaki: "Once Japan lost the war, popular culture had to change. Since it was the adults who lost the war, we couldn't tolerate any more self-important adults. Children, on the other hand, were pure: they bore no responsibility for the war, so we made them our protagonists." And it wasn't simply the young who had to save the world, it was an orphan generation, disenchanted by both adults and the system at large. Tezuka's Atomu may have been abandoned by his creator, but it was this early struggle against adversity that turns him into a hero. In a chapter written in 1967, he sacrifices himself to save a North Vietnamese village from American bombings (before being brought back to life in the next chapter). The father of the mecha genre had already given us the stereotype of (very) young protagonist: in *Tetsujin 28-go*, Mitsuteru Yokoyama (1956) related the adventures of a little boy barely ten years of age. The latter controls the giant titular robot, a secret weapon built by the Japanese imperial army at the end of the war, one which remained unfinished at the time of the surrender. Once reprogrammed, Tetsujin 28-go becomes a force for good. Oh, and the little boy's name? Shotaro Kaneda.

THE IMPACT OF
AKIRA

A MANGA
[R]EVOLUTION

2.2: Creature: The Bosozoku,
Youth in Revolt

T HE CROWDED STREETS OF NEO-TOKYO are riddled with colorful, neon signs. A cloud of pollution shrouds the never-ending traffic. People work and consume. They try to claw their way to the top, above the quagmire, if only to get a bit of fresh air. And within this compliant, consumerist society, young people are running wild, choosing to live a lifestyle that is both profoundly dissolute and self-destructive. With their adrenalin-laden blood pumped full of cheap drugs, they rev the engines of their custom bikes and engage in bloodcurdling fights with rival gangs. Just like in the real Japan of the 1980s, hooligans like Kaneda and Tetsuo cavort under the lights of an empire in the twilight of its collapse.

Akira depicts a youthful generation who crudely rejects any long-term undertaking. With no prospects for the future, their disgust for authority, adults, and rules is almost palpable. And although the air is loaded with carbon, it is this invigorating freedom that allows them to breathe. Tetsuo, Kaneda, Yamagata, and their sidekicks may rule the nighttime streets on their whirring motorcycles, but they live—or rather survive—on the fringes of urban society.

Nevertheless, Kaneda's gang, known as the Capsules, does not live in a totally chaotic world devoid of structure or values. While the gang members reject the adult world, along with the notion of a job, a career, and family responsibilities, they are all part of a codified subculture.[1] Hierarchically organized, it is comprised of a respected leader and the followers who unfailingly obey his orders. It is ultimately this hierarchy that will cause the split between Kaneda and Tetsuo, but we will come back to this later.

When we talk of the Capsules, we are actually speaking about the *bosozoku* (a band of iconic bikers whose cultural heritage has far exceeded the work of Katsuhiro Otomo). They are directly referenced in both the manga and the film. It is important to note that this was a real subculture that appeared in Japan in the 1950s. It peaked in the 1980s, in parallel with the publishing of *Akira*. It would be difficult to come up with a literal rendering of the term *bosozoku*, but the three kanji characters that make up the word (暴走族) speak for themselves: violence (or cruelty), running (or race), and

---

1. Subcultures are not necessarily inferior to mainstream culture.

tribe. As Westerners, we must first shed any preconceived notions we have about biker gangs. Our collective unconscious tends to project the image of a fat, bearded, and graying Hell's Angel. The *bosozoku* were nothing like this. These daredevils were quite young, typically between sixteen and twenty years of age. The reason for this is relatively straightforward: the Japanese can drive two-wheeled vehicles once they turn sixteen. At the time of *Akira*, they could not drive a car until they turned twenty-one (today, the minimum legal age is eighteen). This four-year gap is also the period of transition from adolescence to adulthood: the time during which a boy gradually becomes a man, while nevertheless being spared of the numerous responsibilities inherent in work and family life. Members of the *bosozoku* often did not attend school (through absenteeism, or because they had been expelled), lived with their parents (when the latter were not separated), and came from modest, socially marginal families, generally from the overlooked working class (left on the sidelines by a Japan whose economy was then in the throes of transformation). The flagship documentary about the movement, *God Speed You! Black Emperor* (Mitsuo Yanagimachi, 1976) follows the exploits of a young man who is more or less apathetic in the face of his court summons and his overwhelmed parents. And why should he care about the future? Not only is riding a motorcycle exhilarating, the atmosphere among friends is warm, with everyone laughing as they rush toward the abyss at full speed. One of the Black Emperor members is all smiles when he explains how he nonchalantly introduces himself to a new recruit: "Maybe you know me. I'm Decko. Jobless. I live in a tunnel, no home. I drive better than anybody else. I'll teach you if you want to learn." His bravado is punctuated by the muffled, but not mocking, laughter of his sidekicks. As the sign hanging outside the Harukiya (the bar where Kaneda and his gang regularly hang out) reads: "Abandon all hope, ye who enter." These words—evocative of the Neo-Tokyo reform school where teenagers pretending to care about the future spend more time graffitiing the walls than taking notes—seem to apply to the entire miserable, not to mention ghostly, neighborhood surrounding the bar.

Rejecting authority figures (parents, teachers, police officers, i.e. anyone representing the society they wanted to escape), the *bosozoku* were searching for a world to be a part of, one that recognized their value. This is why there was an element of sport in their activities. Their nocturnal rallies were primarily an opportunity to parade around the city making as much noise as possible. The *bosozoku* thus made their presence known, establishing their turf while sending a hostile message to both city dwellers and rival gangs alike. Because they were out to make an impression, their customized motorcycles (referred to as *kaizosha*) were designed to make them stand out both visually and audibly. The bikes were characterized by high, throne-like seat backs, inwardly curved handlebars, modified (often illegal) engines, flashy colors, and fluttering flags... None of which didn't made them any faster or safer. There was also the rush of defying the Highway Code, since the riders ran red lights, wove around cars, and jeered at Japanese *salarymen* lucky enough to be making their way home, all without wearing any protective gear. And the riders didn't shun such gear because they couldn't afford it, but because they loved taking risks. The *bosozoku* sought danger, excitement, and clashes with law and order to showcase their rebellious nature. And when the police didn't give chase, fights with rival gangs provided the virile adrenaline rush they craved. But since it was all a game of sorts, victories were meaningless and hollow. To have been genuine, the *bosozoku* would have had to have been more violent, better organized, and better armed. They would have had to live in a world that valued more than adolescent reveries. They gave the finger to that which was forbidden to keep their illusions alive, and they let go of the handlebars for a few seconds knowing that they'd grab back onto them to avoid falling. But the excitement was real, and as Carl Jung once said: "Everything you do here, all this, everything, was fantasy to begin with, and fantasy has a proper reality."[2]

Indeed, the notion of theatricality also includes dress codes. In this respect, the bikers in *Akira* do not sport typical *bosozoku* paraphernalia. Instead, they have more of a punk look to them, much like the characters in *Mad Max* (George Miller, 1979) or *The Warriors* (Walter Hill, 1979). The *bosozoku*'s getup of choice was the *tokko-fuku* (特攻服), or "special attack uniform." This name refers to the Japanese World War II kamikaze pilots or *tokko-tai* (特攻隊), i.e. "special attack units," whose gear closely resembled the *bosozoku*'s *tokko-fuku*. This supports Ikuya Sato's analysis,[3] which traces the emergence of the *bosozoku* to the 1950s and the return of young bombers who had not been deployed on suicide missions.[4] To compensate for lost camaraderie and the adrenaline high of danger, these young men formed biker gangs inspired by American films like *Rebel Without a Cause* (Nicholas Ray, 1955), starring the iconic actor James Dean, who personified aimless youth. The inevitable cultural influence of the American occupation also had additional effects, such as introducing Japanese youth to rockabilly, leather jackets, and the pompadour hairstyle, another subculture that lasted long after the Americans themselves had

---

2. Richard I. Evans. *Conversations with Carl Jung & Reactions from Ernest Jones*. D. Van Nostrand Company, Princeton, NJ, 1964.
3. Ikuya Sato. *Kamikaze Biker: Parody and Anomy in Affluent Japan*. University of Chicago Press, 1991.
4. They were also undoubtedly trained in mechanics.

moved on! Over time, the media renamed the motorcycle daredevil gangs (for a time called *kaminarizoku*, or "thunder tribes") *bosozoku*, a name that they readily embraced. Between 1967 and 1972, a series of violent skirmishes between rival gangs inflamed certain prefectures in western Japan. Of these, the Toyama Jiken ("Toyama Incident") attracted the most newspaper attention, seeing as nearly 3,000 people were involved in the large-scale riot (resulting in more than one thousand arrests and considerable material damage). Between 1974 and 1975, similar incidents took place in Kanagawa, a prefecture adjacent to Tokyo, but the pinnacle of violence came in May 1976 during the annual Kobe festival. This time, more than 10,000 people took part in a massive riot, destroying taxis and police cars and setting fire to a police station. Even worse, one group pushed a police truck into a cameraman, who died from his injuries.[5] At the time, the fiercest *bosozoku* wanted to do more than parade around town causing a racket, so they went around smashing cars and shop windows with iron bars. Ironically, it was the resulting media boom that drove many teenagers to join their ranks. In 1973, after episodes like the Toyama Incident, there were approximately 12,500 *bosozoku*. This number swelled to around 42,500 in 1982, at the height of their popularity.[6] Those depicted in *Akira* are clearly extensions of this ultra-violent phase, because only in the most extreme cases did some of the *bosozoku* go on to kidnap or kill their rivals. In Katsuhiro Otomo's futuristic dystopian world, life is cheap, and several young bikers are killed in the streets as of the opening film sequence. The drug use depicted in the manga series was not absent from the world of the *bosozoku* either, but once again, such cases were marginal.[7] The *yakuza* mobsters would sometimes recruit high school students or young men in the *bosozoku* age range to do their dirty work, such as discrete trafficking, but not much else. Due to a code of silence that persists even today, the links between the *bosozoku* and the world of crime remain rather opaque. Nevertheless, they most likely did not surpass the level of petty crime.

Returning to the subject of *bosozoku* paraphernalia, the *tokko-fuku* also reflects another important aspect of the symbolism surrounding the biker gangs: that of a proud, almost arrogant Japan. The *bosozoku* culture was thus often criticized for embodying the militaristic discourse that led to the escalation of conflicts in the Pacific. Many of the bikers' costumes and motorcycles sported war slogans such as "*Zenkoku seiha*" ("Conquer the entire country") and "*Yukoku reishi*" ("Patriotic martyr"), along with more

---

5. Ikuya Sato. *Kamikaze Biker: Parody and Anomy in Affluent Japan.* University of Chicago Press, 1991.
6. This number plummeted to 6,220 in 2017.
7. The young man in *God Speed You! Black Emperor* appears to be a casual user, but the documentary does not pursue the subject.

classic provocations such as "*Nensho joto*" ("F*** juvenile detention") and "*Kenkei dato*" ("Police be damned"). Visual symbols were also quite popular. The Japanese naval flag (also known as the Rising Sun Flag) features a red sun, emitting rays of the same color, on a white background. Neighboring countries, especially those who have suffered from Japanese aggression, often associate it with the Japanese Imperial Army, and it was frequently worn by the *bosozoku*. One of the Capsule members, Yamagata, wears a t-shirt with the motif behind what appears to be Mount Fuji, another symbol of Japanese pride. You could find the rising sun on just about everything: motorcycles, *tokko-fuku*, bandanas, even flags sporting the name of the gang that flew them. But you have to take this nationalist aura with a grain of salt, as the *bosozoku* were essentially apolitical. Street battles were not rooted in fascist desires, and no ideological claims were made. Likewise, there was no sincere nostalgia for Great Imperial Japan. As we have previously mentioned, there was an element of "sport" in the activities of the *bosozoku*. This was referred to as *asobigata hiko*, i.e. play-type delinquency.[8] We are a long way off from Yukio Mishima, who committed suicide after his failed coup d'état in 1970, and this is true even if the first *bosozoku* members of the 1950s were nostalgic proponents of pre-war values (and much more reactionary than their pompadour-sporting successors out for a simple adrenaline rush). Until the 1970s, a popular slogan among young bikers was "*shichisho hokoku*," which means "I wish I had seven lives to give for my country." This legendary tirade was made famous by Kusunoki Masashige, a figure revered by WWII kamikaze pilots (and whose story we shall relate in the next chapter.) It is nevertheless interesting to note that Yukio Mishima also shouted this slogan during his attempted coup d'état! At any rate, there was no staunch alliance between right-wing nationalists and the *bosozoku*. And although it is not uncommon to find a few *bosozoku* members wearing Nazi armbands in various documentaries and archived images (with one gang even calling itself "Hitler"), this was only a means of incitement. One in bad taste, no doubt, but no more than that.

Because the minds of the young suicide bombers were filled with nationalist rhetoric lauding an eternal Japan, it makes sense that their *bosozoku* successors adopted the codes of the feudal era samurai. And the first of these social and behavioral values was a vertical hierarchical structure where everyone has their place and must fully embrace it. When Japan opened itself up to the outside world during the Meiji reform (1868), and even more so after the American occupation, there was a considerable effort on the part of the West to "democratize" relations between the Japanese,

---

8. Ikuya Sato. "Crime as Play and Excitement: Conceptual Analysis of Japanese Bosozoku (Motorcycle Gangs)." *Tohoku Psychologica Folia*, no. 41, 1982.

a desire to "horizontalize" human relations. This had real consequences, particularly in terms of male-female relationships. But in a country that had maintained vertical relations at all levels of society for centuries, it was very difficult to erase old habits, ingrained in the very DNA of people's way of thinking. In this, the *bosozoku*'s nostalgia for the past was also a rebuke aimed at the country's westernization, despite the fact that the bikers also adopted certain American aesthetic codes. Japan is indeed a land of contrasts and contradictions.

The importance of this vertical hierarchy can be seen in the relationship between the bikers and the leader of the group, the *sentosha*, as the latter determines the route and takes the lead while riding around town. The others are not allowed to pass him. Before each outing, "high-ranking" members of the *bosozoku* reviewed their troops and introduced themselves, specifying their position in the hierarchy. Total loyalty to the leader and his comrades was expected. It was part of the moral code inspired by the feudal *bushido* and "sealed" the newcomer in a contract from which it was difficult to disassociate himself. Although this allegiance did not approach the level associated with *yakuza* mobsters, you didn't just waltz in and join a *bosozoku* gang. One had to be ready to help one's comrades in the most desperate of situations, even if this meant being vastly outnumbered in a fight. Discipline was also strict, with leaders backhanding gang members if they made a mistake, much like in the army. But unlike the Capsule members, who line up one-by-one to receive a single punch in the face from their PE teacher (only daring to mock him from a safe distance), the *bosozoku* submitted to the virile authority of their chosen tribe, which they perceived as legitimate (as opposed punishment meted out by adults). This is referred to as *yamato-damashii*, a concept espoused by the *bosozoku*. The expression is difficult to translate into English, since "the spirit of *Yamato*[9]" only covers its literal connotation. More broadly speaking, *yamato-damashii* refers to the idea of a purely Japanese spirit, one that is indomitable and unwavering. While the expression dates back to the Heian period (between 794 and 1185), its warlike aspect was co-opted by the early twentieth century nationalists who assumed power. The phrase was then transformed into a slogan during World War II. The notion included an extreme form discipline mixed with supremacist propaganda, dating back to the end of the nineteenth century when the Japanese Minister of Education declared that "schools were not run for the benefit of the students but for the good of the country."[10] Nationalist mantras were inculcated in young

9. Originally a province where the first emperors supposedly reigned, this was the ancient name for Japan.
10. Anthony Leong. "Those Who Are About To Die: Battle Royale." *Asian Cult Cinema*, no. 33.

students and troops using the same violence as that of the PE teacher, and there were indeed alarming cases of abuse in the army during the Pacific Wars. Several manga artists ridiculed these terrible brainwashing episodes after the war. Despite the subject matter's delicate nature, Shigeru Mizuki did so admirably in *Senso to Nihon (War and Japan)*, where he used graphic violence to parody the sterility of the slogans bellowed into the ears of young recruits.[11] At any rate, it was *yamato-damashii* that drove the Japanese soldiers to grab their bayonets and charge the enemy in one final desperate attack. Capture was synonymous with eternal shame. Their sacrifice and death thus took on a divine, transcendent dimension, since they were giving their lives for something far greater than themselves. Before the charge, the soldiers would shout *"Tennoheika Banzai"* ("Long live His Majesty the Emperor"), a cry that was echoed by the revolutionary who tries to blow himself up with a grenade at the beginning of *Akira* (the film), while Kaneda's gang is being interrogated.[12] This lyrical form of heroism prevented soldiers from questioning their superiors' disastrous battle plans, not to mention the sheer number of lives lost due to logistical errors and the lack of a clear strategy...

Two years before *Akira*, Toshihiro Ishii[13] (a young filmmaker influenced by the punk movement) made the violently polemical *Crazy Thunder Road*, a low-budget movie that has become a cult favorite among genre film fans. Moving beyond the symbolic, it depicted the *bosozoku* and the risks of a potential ideological drift (Ishii had even hired real *bosozoku* rather than professional actors for budgetary reasons). The film stars Jin, a biker spoiling for a fight. He gets caught up in a vengeful downward spiral after one of his sidekicks is killed by a rival gang. Jin becomes involved with an ultra-nationalistic former *bosozoku* who recruits him and some of his gang, thus forming a small militarist group whose admiration for Imperial Japan is strong. Jin ends up asserting his punk spirit when he leaves the group, finding it too sectarian. In the battle to regain his freedom, however, he loses his right hand. Half-crazed, he enters a shady black market that "transforms" him into a kind of low-budget Robocop. After laying his hands on a bazooka, he goes off to kill his former enemies and the aspiring fascists in a final scene as grotesque as it is jubilant. *Crazy Thunder Road* preceded its spiritual sequel *Burst City* by two years. The latter film is even more savage and nihilistic than the former, pioneering a "protocyberpunk" that is closer to *Akira*.

---

11. Among these were: "A good citizen readily sacrifices his life for his emperor!" and "If you have the spirit of *yamato damashii*, you are HUMAN; otherwise you're DIRT, A VILE WORM!" This echoes the propaganda that existed during the Pacific Wars.

12. He makes no mention of an emperor, instead shouting "Long live the revolution, *banzai!*"

13. Better known as Sogo Ishii, a pseudonym that he would eventually swap for Gakuryu Ishii in 2012.

The year that *Weekly Young Magazine* published the first chapter of *Akira* was also the year that the *bosozoku* reached its apogee in terms of membership. The rebel wave then began to ebb, never to rise again (at least not in the same form). The Japanese youth of the 1980s would also come to embrace self-gratification, but it came in the form of overconsumption instead of self-destruction. Manga, as a whole, had mostly lost the left-leaning progressive edge championed by the veterans. It no longer fulfilled its antisystemic role: the industry was turning into a cash machine that nothing seemed to thwart, and publishers were exerting more and more pressure on the creative types. Members of the new generation, who did not have assistants and small personal businesses like the manga artists of yesteryear, produced what they were allowed to produce.

And then, as the rebellious *bosozoku* became increasingly insignificant, the streets of Tokyo gave way to a new type of free spirit, radically different and yet also a product of its time: the *shinjinrui* generation (新人類). This term, coined in 1985, literally means "a new breed" and refers to Japanese people who grew up during and after the 1970s. In essence, they never experienced the difficulties of the post-war period, being born at a time when Japan was already well on its way to becoming an "economic miracle." This generation inherited a rebuilt Japan with a bright, shiny future. While the common good and the group were once more important than personal desires, a new individuality was emerging. In fact, a survey of about 3,000 young people conducted by the NHK in the late 1980s showed that 55% of them "considered their own welfare before that of society."[14] While the previous generation had rolled up their sleeves, working their fingers to the bone to buy the three "sacred treasures of Japan"[15] (the television, the washing machine, and the refrigerator), the *shinjinrui* took these conveniences for granted and instead coveted a nice car and enough money to dine out at nice restaurants. Karyn Poupée evokes this economic "bubble culture" when she specifies that "all young people dreamed of a career as a trader or creative type in television, advertising, fashion magazines, entertainment, or art, i.e. a career path opposite that of their predecessors, who were engineers, technicians, researchers, or workers."[16] The discrepancy between underprivileged youth and those able to afford the bling-bling lifestyle is portrayed in *Akira*. During the

14. Susan Chira. "Tokyo Journal; Motto for a New Breed: Less Work and More Play." *The New York Times*, 25 Jan. 1988.
15. A reference to the three legendary treasures of Japan (the Kusanagi-no-Tsurugi sword, the Yata-no-Kagami mirror, and the Yasakani-no-Magatama jewel), offered to the first emperors by the gods.
16. Karyn Poupée. *Les Japonais*. Éd. Tallandier, expanded edition of January 2015.

film's opening sequence, one of the bikers crashes into a fancy restaurant where well-dressed young people are enjoying a quiet evening out. Having seen the bikers weaving through the streets, the man in the suit had just cracked an edifying comment: "Hmph, young people today!" In the world of *Akira*, misery, despair, and those out for an adrenaline rush turn the posh neighborhoods upside down. Status symbols and luxury goods topple to the ground, depicting the meeting of two increasingly distant worlds, whose relationship becomes one of contempt (and even antagonism). While the Japan of the 1980s was not Neo-Tokyo, the climate toward the end of the decade nevertheless shared a number of commonalities with it. The real estate golden boys, who didn't know what to do with all of their money in the early nineties, were about to see their world collapse when the speculative bubble burst, thus putting an end to the post-war dream and signaling the beginning of the troubles that gave birth to the famous "lost generation."

Akira's description of a Japan that had run its course was prophetic: it locked its neuroses in cold storage and hid its social inequalities under successive advertising campaigns that vomited out their frenzied exhortations to consume on every street corner. Otomo finished the series in June 1990, when the Japanese speculative bubble was about to burst, resulting in more than just an economic crisis. It was a crisis of meaning that really shook Japan, a crisis whose after-effects can still be felt today. In concrete terms, the model of the lifelong *salaryman* collapsed. Many young people no longer saw the point of knocking themselves out to pass the excruciating university entrance exams (and then there was the growing problem of bullying [*ijime*], which was generally covered up by school administrations). This backdrop led to the emergence of a generation of *freeters* (*furita*), young people who eked out a living doing odd jobs, and *neets* (*nito*), school dropouts who remained unemployed. This was compounded by growing school absenteeism (not to mention the beginning of the *hikkikomori* phenomenon, with recluses confining themselves in their homes for years). The traditional family unit also broke up, with the divorce rate almost doubling between 1990 and 2002, thus creating a new class of poor single mothers... To make matters even worse, the Japanese witnessed a considerable upsurge in teenage violence that shocked the public at large, particularly when a fourteen-year-old killed two children, aged ten and eleven, in Kobe in 1997. The head of one of these youngsters was left in plain view in front of his school, with a note signed by the murderer stuck in his mouth. The perpetrator said that he "desperately wanted to see people die to relieve years of great bitterness." And ultimately, in 1998, suicide became the sixth leading cause of death in Japan, with nearly 31,000 fatalities (a 35% increase over the previous year).[17]

The "lost generation" merited its name. The previous generation's excesses had pushed Japanese society toward a "more and more" mentality that was impossible to sustain beyond the short term. In *Little Boy*, an exhibition dedicated to the legacy of atomic imagery in post-war Japanese culture, Takashi Murakami compared the atmosphere of *Akira*'s Neo-Tokyo to that of Japan at the time of the manga's publication: "In this unprecedented economic expansion, Japan's urban landscape underwent rapid and fundamental changes through rezoning, as real-estate speculation ran rampant in cities throughout the country. The Tokyo ravaged by these real-life capitalist forces was not so different from the post-Armageddon Tokyo depicted in the manga. A vague sense of end-of-the-century anxiety, the hope of escaping the coming catastrophe, and the longing for some supernatural power that would bring about salvation–in other words, the zeitgeist of the 1980s–were imaginatively folded into *Akira*."

As we have seen in the previous chapter, young protagonists are quite popular in both manga and animation. From Tezuka's *Astro Boy* to the young *Gundam* novice pilots, the generational divide has always been present, especially in stories whose subtext refers to WWII history or an imminent holocaust. This emphasis on youth mixes hope with revolutionary discourse. After all, the best way to avoid repeating the mistakes of the past is to give birth to a generation that is more responsible than the previous one.

Otomo is indeed a revolutionary at heart. And given that the *bosozoku* actually existed in Japan in the 1980s, his inspiration for *Akira* was not all that fanciful! But the manga artist was also influenced by another movement in his youth, one that had an even greater political, social, and cultural impact than that of the raucous bikers: the Japanese student movement of the late 1960s. During this period, students around the world seemed to be calling for a widespread revolt. And while their demands were not always well defined, their mobilization made the headlines at a time when the war of images was gearing up, thanks to the increasing prevalence of television sets.

Nonetheless, Japan's case was unique. In addition to problems within the universities themselves, one of the major causes of student mobilization was the forthcoming renewal of the Mutual Cooperation and Security Treaty concluded between the US and Japan in 1960.[18] Its signature had already

---

17. *Ibid.*
18. A treaty of mutual security and collaboration, introducing the notion of reciprocity.

led to massive protests that included the Zengakuren (the All-Japan Federation of Student Self-Government Associations), whose members paraded around armed with bamboo sticks and helmets fastened to their heads.

A large percentage of the Japanese population believed that the treaty was an impediment to peace and a justification for involving Japan in the United States' wars. Locals were vehemently against turning the archipelago into a service station for the US Air Force, decrying the idea that the Americans could simply drop in before going on to bomb neighboring countries. Throughout the 1960s, Japan saw apolitical movements aimed at promoting peace and denouncing the American imperialist cavalcade as well as the escalation of the war in Vietnam. In 1965, the latter gave rise to the Beheiren group,[19] which was popular with students. Like many of the manga artists of their era, Japanese students were primarily left-leaning. While Todai University[20] students were singing *The Internationale* and adorning the prestigious institution's famous red door with a portrait of Chinese Cultural Revolution leader Mao Zedong and the slogan "*Teidai kaitai*" ("Dismantle the imperial university"), one of *Doraemon*'s authors, Motoo Abiko,[21] was penning a manga biography of this very same leader, whose ideas found a favorable echo in the universities. Karl Marx's opposition between we and them, the oppressor and the oppressed, was hitting home with a large segment of the Japanese youth. Yet it would be wrong to think that these students were big fans of the Soviet Union. It was the world order that they rejected, as the US-USSR binarity forced the rest of the world to engage in a dangerous game of alliances. During this era, there was talk of a "New Left" in Japan. This was a reaction to the Old Left, which had become too corporatist, with rigid political alliances and ideologies that could only promote a phony facade of peace. The essence of the revolt revolved around the very idea of revolt: all power structures, be it the universities themselves, the political parties, or the intelligentsia, were criticized for what they were, i.e. structures. This was what led to the rise of the student movement as well as its inevitable fall: the struggle was ultimately futile because it was too abstract. The youth uprising cannot be fully attributed to social concerns, such as the lack of democratic functioning in universities, the cost of college enrollment, the Vietnam War, or the Japan-US security treaty. These were outgrowths of a deeper desire: the students criticized these structures and events because, in their view, they were leading to uniformization. The latter was dispossessing citizens

19. Short for Betonamu ni Heiwa wo Shimin Rengo, or Citizens' League for Peace in Vietnam.
20. Abbreviation for Tokyo Daigaku, i.e. the University of Tokyo.
21. Abiko was one half of a writing duo known as Fujiko Fujio that included his collaborator Hiroshi Fujimoto. They parted ways in 1987, but Abiko continued to use the duo's name, signing his work "Fujiko Fujio A."

of their individuality, at a time when capitalism was radically changing Japanese society and leading it toward a questionable future.

It is estimated that at the height of the movement, in 1969, 152 of Japan's 370 universities were demonstration hotbeds. Even Todai University professors were not exempt. These once-revered figures, admired for their knowledge and vocation, were becoming targets of gratuitous attacks and accusations of collusion with a "fascistic" government (several of them even committed suicide). Students sought a sacrosanct convergence of causes behind barricaded buildings, under tents, and between haphazardly erected banners, even if their grievances often had nothing to do with one another. And yet in their radicalism, the various student groups rejected the shackles of ideology. For instance, they also denounced the aging rhetoric of the Japanese Communist Party and the automatism of their indignation (the Party had strong ties to the USSR, which did not help matters any). But deconstruction and renunciation aren't enough. To achieve progress, a foundation must be laid. In a 1969 publication, Makoto Oda (one of Beheiren's founders) warned that Japanese university fees and the Vietnam War should not be conflated.[22] Students' demands regarding their milieu were, by the way, perfectly legitimate: universities were welcoming an exponential number of new arrivals (with 20% of secondary school graduates attending college in 1968 as opposed to only 8% in 1960), making competition much fiercer while no longer guaranteeing a smooth entry into the workforce. Unsurprisingly, the declining quality of education, which students saw as a "mass product" unworthy of the cost of tuition, was eventually blamed. Freedom of thought in education became an important cause from the 1990s onward. During this same period, the aging bureaucracy of French universities was described as "Napoleonic" (i.e. ridiculously outdated).[23]

It is also important to remember that more and more Japanese households were equipping themselves with televisions at the time. The images of masked students pontificating underneath banners—amidst revolutionary slogans, no less—had a rather spectacular effect. The youngest among them seemed almost jubilant. And as surprising as it may seem to us Westerners, the majority of Japanese people (including politicians) actually approved of their uprising! As an appreciative childhood spectator of these riots, it is hardly surprising that Katsuhiro Otomo showed similar images on the Harukiya bar's television early in the film. We see violent demonstrations against tax reforms that have put many Neo-Tokyoites out

22. John L. Tran. "1968: The Year Japan Truly Raised its Voice." *The Japan Times*, 19 Nov. 2017.
23. Eiji Oguma. "What Was 'The 1968 Movement?' Japan's Experience in a Global Perspective." *The Asia-Pacific Journal: Japan Focus*, vol. 16, 1 June 2018.

of work. Color television, which was still relatively novel during the time of the student revolts, helped to construct the superbly seductive aura that surrounded them. And the students were all too happy to cooperate: the news stations' media coverage was the perfect way to promote their cause, so they deliberately tried to attract the attention of cameramen with their brightly colored helmets. After all, they had been seeing student protests breaking out all over the world for months! In 1967, the police cracked down on a small group of activists attempting to prevent Prime Minister Eisaku Sato from traveling to South Vietnam. Images of the scuffle, which occurred near Tokyo's Haneda Airport, were broadcast in homes throughout the entire country. And since one person was killed, the halo of "martyrdom" supplemented the adrenaline rush that accompanied the call to arms. The revolts turned into urban guerrilla warfare the following year, with the so-called "Shinjuku riots" involving tens of thousands of young people (not just students either)! Workers, both blue-and white-collar, joined the rioters. Could they have been driven by the *bosozoku* need to feel alive?

Eiji Oguma, a professor at Keio University in Tokyo, suggests that these uprisings were about more than warring factions and their grievances. He sees them as a reaction to the dehumanization brought about by the country's economic boom and to the gap between the rosy picture painted by the universities and the harsh reality awaiting students. In addition to a bright future, newcomers expected to enjoy a certain status. Instead, the sad gray buildings built to accommodate the growing number of students– who were packed into amphitheaters where individuality was drowned out–disenchanted even the most optimistic among them. Adding to this trend, the rapid transformation to an increasingly consumeristic society tended to baffle many of the Japanese. Recalling a young housewife's musings, Oguma wrote about the apprehension of the times: "Suddenly we were getting richer and richer. We could buy washing machines and TVs, but we felt extremely uneasy. We kept thinking, is this okay? Is this really okay?"[24] Wealth caused, or at the very least did not resolve, the crisis of meaning experienced by the Japanese, who were dealing with all of this for the very first time. And, well, let's face it: throwing rocks at the police turned out to be surprisingly entertaining.

Various student groups and associations unofficially banded together to form an overarching alliance called Zenkyoto,[25] a nebulous informal system beyond the control and endorsement of traditional student organizations

24. Eiji Oguma. "Japan's 1968: A Collective Reaction to Rapid Economic Growth in an Age of Turmoil." *The Asia-Pacific Journal: Japan Focus*, vol. 13, 23 May 2015.
25. Abbreviation for Zengaku Kyoto Kaigi, aka All-Campus Joint Struggle Council.

(Zengakuren) and their pyramidal hierarchies. These conventional organizations were no less structured than the old political parties and were thus becoming just as obsolete. But this hostility to structure is exactly what nipped the movement in the bud. Despite Zenkyoto's impressive membership, it was incapable of establishing any guiding principles (or even achieving internal peace). And the universities no longer hesitated to recruit far-right-wing manpower to sabotage the insurgents' gatherings, sometimes enlisting the help of PE faculty members. Hey, why not?

One of the first blows to the movement was the renewal of the Japan-US Security Treaty in 1970, which clearly undermined the students' revolutionary aspirations. Japan's self-determination was crippled, and the status quo that had prevailed prior to the demonstrations was strengthened. More and more students, the younger ones in particular, ended up embracing consumer culture by adopting very American fads: they listened to rock music, sported pompadours, and went to see Hollywood films. Ultimately, they came to accept and appreciate the excellent economic prospects and general rise in the standard of living. Later, those who were more determined became radical, moving from rocks to Molotov cocktails and from slogans to hostage-taking: the police hardened their stance, and 2,000 students were arrested. The United Red Army, formed in 1971, embodied this sectarian and ultra-violent trend by executing members who were "not sufficiently revolutionary": twelve members were killed between December 31, 1971 and February 12, 1972, profoundly shocking the Japanese public. Prior to this, on March 31, 1970, another radical group known as the Japanese Communist League–Red Army Faction (a predecessor of the Japanese Red Army) hijacked Japan Airlines Flight 351 while flying from Tokyo to Fukuoka, taking a total of 129 hostages. Before the plane's take-off from Fukuoka (where 21 hostages were released), the terrorists reportedly shouted: "We are *Ashita no Joe!*" They finally landed in South Korea, where they accepted the plea of Japan's Vice Minister for Transport (who volunteered to take the place of the remaining hostages). With the Vice Minister in tow, they took off for Pyongyang, North Korea and were granted political asylum. Worse still, the Japanese Red Army was responsible for the massacre at Lod Airport (now Ben Gurion International Airport) near Tel Aviv: twenty-six people were killed and eighty were wounded. This quashed any further talk of peaceful demonstrations, not to mention heckling, as the Japanese public no longer recognized the cause that they had overwhelmingly supported.

Ashita no Joe, the boxing manga illustrated by Tetsuya Chiba, had found a particular resonance in the student movements of the late 1960s. The "fight culture" is perfectly embodied by Joe, an orphaned boxer who has what can only be described as a hard-knock life. The manga's cultural impact cannot be overstated: after the death of one of its most emblematic characters, Rikiishi (who is both Joe's rival and role model), a "real" funeral was held and attended by a crowd of nearly 700 fans. The imaginary character's death was even reported in the newspaper *Tokyo Chunichi Sports*![26] It was Rikiishi and Joe's indomitable fighting spirit that resonated among the barricaded demonstrators, inspiring them to paint vitriolic slogans on banners and call for the overthrow of the old regime. The means hardly mattered. Nor did the outcome. The "fight," in and of itself, was enough for the protesters, who scorned future prospects, authority, aging structures, the promises of adults, and the "system" at large. They wanted to exist as actors, not become a number or body lost in the masses. *Ashita no Joe* ends on a bittersweet note. By decision of the judges, Joe loses his last fight against the terrible Jose Mendoza, the unbeatable world champion against whom Joe has played fifteen rounds characterized by unprecedented violence. The young man had begun the match with a serious handicap, since his previous fights had left him punch-drunk[27] and completely blind in one eye. But his defeat was ultimately glorious, even if it was in vain! As soon as Mendoza's victory is announced, his hair turns white, as if he is now one of the "old boys," who needs to make way for a generation that, despite its inexperience, is ready to die in the ring for its right to exist. The last image of the manga shows Joe unconscious on his stool. He looks peaceful, with the ghost of a smile playing on his lips. Is he dead? In all likelihood. But the fight made him feel alive, truly and genuinely alive. His coach murmurs to him that he fought well, while Yoko (who has fallen in love with Joe) asks for his gloves, which are still dripping with the blood of his opponent. A real Zenkyoto activist was quoted as saying: "Life is empty, and the future is hopeless. We wear helmets, carry wooden sticks, and confront death. In that moment, at the very least, one should experience some feeling of being alive."[28]

The *bosozoku*, the rioting students, and Kaneda's gang have all that particular sentiment in common. Because there is an element of "sport" in their sacrosanct quest for adrenaline, tomorrow is of little importance. They do not take the future seriously (perhaps because they know that their struggle is in vain). Their unrest is spurious, a symptom of deep malaise that cannot be cured by reforms or political manifestos. As for Kaneda,

---

26. Karyn Poupée. *Histoire du Manga*. Éd. Tallandier, June 2016.
27. Caused by repeated concussive and sub-concussive injuries to the head, punch drunk syndrome is also referred to as "chronic traumatic encephalopathy" or "dementia pugilistica." It is believed that this condition may have contributed to Mohamed Ali's Parkinson's disease.
28. Eiji Oguma. "Japan's 1968: A Collective Reaction to Rapid Economic Growth in an Age of Turmoil." *The Asia-Pacific Journal: Japan Focus*, vol. 13, 23 May 2015.

Tetsuo, and their sidekicks, their mad rush toward self-destruction is even more striking. Gorging themselves on cheap drugs without worrying about the latter's long-term effects, they blithely mock the reprimands of officials telling them that this is "their last chance to become good citizens" [29] and engage in bloody battles against equally hedonistic gangs. As opposed to the film, it is the manga's conclusion that ultimately drives the nail into the coffin of *carpe diem*: Kaneda refuses the offer of international (and particularly American) aid, which is needed to help rebuild Japan and care for the wounded. Kaneda rejects the olive branch that is being offered, preferring to go it alone, even if he has no particular objective in mind. He doesn't rush toward tomorrow, but toward today, the present moment where he has always felt most free. At the end of *Crazy Thunder Road*, the protagonist, Jin, hits the road on a motorcycle without brakes. When someone points this out to him, he replies: "Where I'm going, I don't need them."

Revolt tends to have this universal value, whose echoes reverberate in the most unlikely places. In her book *Anime, from Akira to Howl's Moving Castle: Experiencing Contemporary Japanese Animation*, Susan J. Napier recounts the story of an unexpected sight, encountered by Japanese critic Toshiya Ueno during his visit to Sarajevo, in war-torn Serbia, in 1993: "In the middle of the old city was a crumbling wall with three panels. On the first, [there was] a picture of Mao Zedong with Mickey Mouse ears; the second had a slogan for the Chiapas liberation group (the Zapatistas) emblazoned on it. But when he came to the third, he was at a loss for words. Incredibly, it was a large panel of a scene from Otomo Katsuhiro's *Akira*. Against the crumbling walls of the collapsing group of buildings, that 'mighty juvenile delinquent' Kaneda was saying 'So it's begun!'"

Returning to the real *bosozoku*, they haven't disappeared (at least not entirely). But the recession of the 1990s, falling wages, and rising unemployment made it more difficult for the poorer classes to afford and maintain a motorcycle. And fewer and fewer people wore the *tokko-fuku*, given that the garment was rather expensive. In addition, a drastic tightening of measures taken by the police, who began to compile individual files thanks to their vehicles' cameras, undermined the recklessness that prevailed in the major urban processions of the 1970s and 80s. And while young bikers were once released with a flick on the wrist, Big Brother now took on the task of maintaining order. From 2004 onward, following the passage of a new traffic law, anyone resembling a *bosozoku* was immediately stopped, and any breach of the law resulted in a hefty fine. It was no longer a laughing matter.

---

29. In the manga, Yamagata lashes out at a teacher whose "deafening" moral lesson prevents the young man from reading the race results.

Ikuya Sato has suggested another rationale for the disappearance of motorcycle gangs: their popularity. He believes that their entry into pop culture robbed them of their rebel appeal. And *Akira* is by no means a stranger to this phenomenon! The incredible triumph of Katsuhiro Otomo, who had a major role in the export of manga outside of Japan, brought the *bosozoku*, along with their symbols and attitudes, into a realm that no longer had much to do with a marginal and antisystemic subculture. And, as we have previously mentioned, the year of *Akira*'s publication, 1982, was the height of *bosozoku*'s membership. As soon as a subculture becomes mainstream, it loses its explosive power and (in the worst case scenario) becomes an echo of its former self. The recent revival of eighties pop culture hasn't helped matters any. The success of *Stranger Things*, *Ready Player One*, [30] retrogaming, synthwave, and projects that rely on crowdfunding (such as *Kung Fury*) demonstrate a strong appetite for the "aesthetics of the '80s," and it's not uncommon to come across millennials wearing an *Akira* t-shirt or even a reproduction of Kaneda's jacket. Isn't it ironic that Otomo plastered Kaneda's motorcycle—which has become a real artifact of pop culture—with stickers promoting Canon, Shoei, and Arai helmets? In cyberpunk cities, where consumer capitalism is constantly seeking new ways to advertise, hasn't Kaneda's motorcycle also become an elite "product" hiding behind its red antisystemic facade?

30. The character Art3mis drives Kaneda's motorcycle in a race featuring pop culture vehicles.

THE IMPACT OF
AKIRA

A MANGA
[R]EVOLUTION

2.3: Creature: Tetsuo
(First Phase)

A *KIRA* IS A FRAGMENTED TALE, composed of intertwining plots and subplots. Katsuhiro Otomo's masterpiece thus rejects the "classical" narrative structure, i.e. one in which the protagonist faces a challenge and, in overcoming it, becomes a better version of himself. As the story's fictional characters come to a crossroads, their fate will depend on how they react to an artifact (Akira), one that is either feared, coveted, adored, or abhorred. The absence of a unifying central character frees up the narrative's dramatic arcs, rendering them more malleable. It thus becomes less necessary to have the characters "evolve" as human beings. This partly explains *Akira*'s classification as a "post-modern" work. It is similar to the film *Pulp Fiction*, whose storylines intermingle and prevent viewers from guessing the final outcome (if there even is a bona fide outcome).

Fans who first saw the animated film version of *Akira* must have been surprised when they finally got around to reading the manga. After all, Kaneda is totally absent for about a quarter of the series (as is Tetsuo, although not concomitantly). The manga makes it clearer that Kaneda's role is primarily one of comic relief. Despite all his "heroic" risk-taking, he never really takes center stage. And while the stakes grow ever higher—from attempting to win a gang war to potentially saving the world—Kaneda remains more or less the same. His goal is to stop Tetsuo and win Kei's heart. His stubborn resolve is what makes him sympathetic, since he consistently ignores (and insults) all the authority figures in his way, from Colonel Shikishima to Lady Miyako. It is his unbelievable audacity, bordering on recklessness, that puts him in grave danger. And yet, it is this same quality that gets him out of trouble time and time again. From beginning to end, Kaneda remains Kaneda: an uncontrollable and insolent young daredevil who survives an apocalypse without becoming even a tad bit more responsible.

With the possible exception of Kei, Tetsuo is the only character who truly evolves throughout the tale, both psychologically and physically (or, more accurately, metaphysically). He embodies nearly all of *Akira*'s themes: adolescence, generational conflict, the destruction of the social fabric, the lust for power, military experimentation, loss of control, tribalism, despair, and so forth. But unlike the mysterious briefcase in *Pulp Fiction*, Tetsuo is not reduced to an impotent MacGuffin[1] around whom the rest of the cast revolves. Tetsuo confronts Neo-Tokyo's various factions, eventually defying and sometimes destroying them, while undergoing the effects of his metamorphosis. And these effects are the outgrowths of something much larger, as they are the direct result of the city's evils. Tetsuo is at the center of a complex web, linking various groups and beliefs. It is thus imperative to analyze his multiphase transformation.

Not much is known about the teenager's early life. Neither the manga nor the film offer more than fragmented clues, suggesting an extremely disturbed childhood and one (or perhaps several) toxic home environments. While the film portrays him as an orphan, who was most likely abandoned, the manga references a "mother." In a nebulous flashback, readers see a woman who says she's fed up with his wayward behavior and that he "isn't even her real son." Kaneda comes from a similar background, but he appears to be both stronger and more extroverted than the shy Tetsuo. He rapidly assumes the role of the latter's protective big brother. And despite the fact that Tetsuo obviously depends on Kaneda, the former is eventually reminded of his own weakness, which he finds increasingly difficult to shoulder. Tetsuo's frustration drives him to commit excessive acts of violence.

The true origins of his resentment remain unclear, but it is possible that Kaneda simply went overboard, acting too much like a parental figure. The leader of the Capsules seems to have taken on several roles at once: that of an admirable big brother, a protective mother, and a courageous father. His relationship with Tetsuo is one-sided, and this vertical hierarchy eventually weighs on his sidekick. It is also likely that Tetsuo joined the Capsules as Kaneda's protégé and that, as such, he did not need to prove his worth through a diverse range of "macho" exploits. Their relationship undoubtedly began to shift as they entered adolescence. During this stage, the ego develops and pride blooms, resulting in virile competitions, especially when there is a female audience in attendance. The relationship between the protector and the protected becomes suffocating for the latter, who is treated like a child.

Tetsuo's initial outbursts are benign, and therefore tolerable to the pack leader. The Capsules are amused by the young man's risky behavior when it doesn't cause them concern. After all, he is far from being the strongest gang member. They laugh at his stunts the way they would laugh at a

---

1. Something that the protagonists of a fictional work want to get their hands on. It may be an object or a person. Its nature remains unclear and serves as a trigger for the plot (allowing the story to move forward).

puppy's bark. And although he rides his bike at maximum speed, Tetsuo is well aware that Kaneda has a bigger one. In the film, Tetsuo even manages to steal his friend's bike, but he finds himself unable to control it. The symbolism is apparent, without any further explanation being needed.

He becomes openly hostile toward Kaneda upon his initial return from the military hospital. The Capsule leader comes to his rescue when he is attacked by a rival gang, known as the Clowns. Enraged by this turn of events, Tetsuo begins to attack a fallen assailant, with the intent to kill. When Kaneda tells his friend to stop, a rebellious Tetsuo retorts: "I don't take orders from you." We have already discussed the rigid rules espoused by the *bosozoku* in the last chapter, i.e. the mandate to respect a vertical hierarchy and follow the gang leader's orders. Tetsuo's refusal to obey is not just an affront to Kaneda. It is also a dangerous transgression of the moral and social order and, as such, concerns the entire group. In the manga, this fractured relationship is shown via a clear symmetry that opposes the two friends. The panels resemble a poster for a boxing match, with the determined opponents stoically facing off.

In the end, this surge of pride passes. But what Tetsuo eventually does goes far beyond an exceptional slip. It cannot be swept under the rug by an apology. In the manga, the young man is once again attacked by the Clowns, but the fight's second round has a very different outcome. Tetsuo's nascent powers enable him to easily repel and vanquish his opponents. He then turns the situation to his advantage. Needing drugs to alleviate his terrible migraines, the teen demands that he be taken to the Clowns' headquarters, where he feasts on a buffet of narcotics. Unfortunately, the cheap drugs circulating among the gangs don't have much of an effect, even when taken in massive doses. Tetsuo then displaces the Joker as the Clowns' leader. He immediately orders his minions to steal drugs from rival gangs.

He remorselessly attacks his former friends, a moral fault that the *bosozoku*—in the manner of old feudal Japan—cannot forgive. In Japanese culture, clan mentality plays a much more fundamental role than it does in the West: it rules all social interactions, right down to the notion of morality itself. The clan's rules determine right from wrong, with even truth being relegated to the back burner. The world is divided into *ie* or *uchi* (the in-group) and *soto* (the out group), in other words *us* versus *them*. This is one of the reasons why critical thinking came late to Japan: the words of one's superior, all the way up to the emperor as the supreme incarnation, were supposed to be both just and unquestionable, making it difficult to untangle the truth from lies. Historical documents point to a telling distinction between Chinese and Japanese emperors. The Chinese described all of their dynasties' deeds, both good and bad, fostering critical thinking skills. This was not true of the Japanese, whose emperor remained divine and, as such, the moral arbitrator of the nation.[2] The same was true of the many Buddhist sects. Entire families belonged to one or another, and the oppositions between them were not based on religious or intellectual disagreements, but on whether or not they belonged to the "right" sect.[3] The clan was both a mental and social matrix, and although this concept was undermined by the Meiji Reformation, the American occupation and, ultimately, the bursting of the economic bubble in the early 1990s, it still seems impossible for the Japanese to completely separate themselves from this way of thinking. Even after the 1945 defeat and the supposed downfall of the traditional values touted by the military dictatorship, corporations—with their offer of "lifelong employment"—became the heirs of this time-honored clannism. When the Japanese present a business card, as they tend to do indiscriminately, they are first introducing themselves as a clan member. Their position in the hierarchy is secondary. In the professional realm, this is known as *marugakae*, a term that essentially means "total involvement." It suggests that employees must give their whole being to the company. This does not imply servitude: it underscores the notion that individual identity melds into clan affiliation. The same was true for feudal Japan's samurai and *daimyo* (lords), with stories of eternal loyalty being commonplace in the literature of the era. *The Taiheiki* (*Chronicle of Great Peace*), written in the late 14th century, serves as a good example. Totally devoted to his emperor Go-Daigo (1288-1339), Kusunoki Masashige (1294-1336) is trapped in a losing battle. He addresses his brother one last time, asking him what he would want if he were to be reincarnated. The brother replies that he would like to live seven times and continue to serve his lord, which Masashige obviously approves of, although it is not a very Buddhist-like sentiment. The two then commit harakiri. It is hardly surprising that Masashige's sense of sacrifice served as a totem for WWII Japanese suicide bombers (and, in the previous chapter, we have seen how closely their codes resemble those of the *bosozoku*). Unwavering loyalty, in defiance of death and even reason (in the manner of the *Yamato* crew who entered into battle knowing that they were on a one-way mission), is considered the ultimate virtue and still resounds centuries later in hearts of those who dream of a heroic demise.

In Japan, it is customary to say that "no man can serve two masters." This is logical if you understand the importance of the clan and its vertical

2. Hajime Nakamura. *Ways of Thinking of Eastern Peoples: India, China, Tibet, Japan.* University of Hawaii Press, 1981.
3. Indian Buddhists were much more versed in debating opposing points of view pertaining to religious matters. But the Japanese took what they wanted from Buddhism, which had already been transformed by its journey through China and Korea.

hierarchy. Even the *bosozoku* had a procedure for joining and leaving the group. In *God Speed You! Black Emperor*, the viewer witnesses a scene showing a young gang member being knocked around by his pals. This is because his actions have conveyed uncertainty about his membership in the group. He isn't being mistreated because he wants to go it alone, he is being "punished" for letting the other members down. He can leave, but he can't just run away. Things have to been done by the book.

As for Tetsuo, he thwarts all the rules. His trampling of them is one of the main reasons that Kaneda becomes angry when he learns that his friend has taken over leadership of the Clowns. In Japan, moving from one clan to another is a transgression, and all parties feel it. If you join a company that is in competition with the one you just left, it will be extremely difficult for you to find your place in the new one. This is because you belong to the out-group, or *soto*, and your arrival disrupts the homogeneity of the in-group, or *ie*.[4] By leaving secretively, Tetsuo indirectly declares war on Kaneda, the one person that had protected him for years (Kaneda was basically Tetsuo's *senpai* or even *oyabun*). Even worse, Tetsuo did so without shame. In contrast, Kaneda is well aware of his responsibilities. When he learns of Tetsuo's desertion, the Capsules encourage him to fight back. Their leader's response is an appropriate one: "Yes dammit! It's a matter of principle! No self-respecting biker lets a bunch of junkies kick his ass!"

It is also this notion of the common good (i.e. that of the clan) that prevents managers, leaders, bosses, and landowners from becoming too avaricious. Even though Japanese society is based on a vertical hierarchy, those who find themselves at the bottom of the clan's ladder are not to be belittled. They are part of the group, and that's all that matters. They are entitled to feel just as proud as those at the top. And indeed, it is rare to see a higher-up's greed go so far as to risk hurting the group at large. In Japan, an entrepreneur who puts his personal gain ahead of group honor and continuity will face a greater backlash than he would in more individualistic Western countries, where the boss would "merely" be accused of profiteering and move on to find a job elsewhere. The taint of scandal is much harder to shake in Japanese society. On the other hand, if a business leader has lied, been deceitful, or otherwise acted in a manner contrary to our Western morality, but has done so for the good of the clan, the Japanese would be more likely to forgive and forget.

---

4. This does not mean that the relationship between groups is unfriendly. The Japanese people's legendary politeness (which is also very codified) means that people speak of their group humbly and show respect for that of their interlocutor.

These cultural values underscore the fact that Tetsuo behaves in the worst possible way when he becomes the new leader of the Clowns (something that only occurs in the manga). Not only does he siphon off the Clowns' resources for his own profit, he also ends up leading them into an all-out war with the rest of Neo-Tokyo's gangs. This conflict primarily involves massive looting, with the stolen goods going to Tetsuo alone. He even goes so far as to tell his brand new "friends": "The only reason you're still alive is because I let you live." In a land of many contradictions, the *bosozoku* themselves embodied a paradox. They sought to be agents of chaos while holding on to a well-established social structure: their own. Tetsuo, on the other hand, is both nihilistic and selfish. His neurotic impulses drive him to destroy everything that stands in the way of his pride and personal pleasure. This is the beginning of Tetsuo's downfall, for his capriciousness will come back to haunt him.

THE IMPACT OF AKIRA

AKIRA

A MANGA [R]EVOLUTION

2.4: Creature: Cyberpunk and Japan, the Body from Every Angle

AKIRA IS OFTEN DESCRIBED AS one of the pioneering works of the cyberpunk genre, much like Ridley Scott's film *Blade Runner* (1982) and William Gibson's novel *Neuromancer* (1984). After all, manga, film, and literature often overlap and influence one another. This is why any attempt to determine the origin of cyberpunk is like playing an eternal game of "who influenced whom," a war of suppositions and hypotheses that rarely results in anything concrete, especially given that the genre seems to have been born on different continents at the same time. Consequently, cyberpunk is viewed as the natural evolution of science fiction, a subgenre which, while projecting the reader/viewer into a not necessarily near future, remains the product of an era that saw the world changing at breakneck speed, with technology taking an increasingly invasive place in daily life.

Cyberpunk is thus an offshoot of science fiction and is essentially based on the notion of technological progress. The classic cyberpunk setting is a megalopolis, one in which large corporations have appropriated political power while consumer capitalism has revamped the urban landscape. Enticing advertisements are found everywhere. They are, quite literally, unavoidable. The city's population has succumbed to a form of consumer hedonism which, combined with advances in science and technology, has opened up new sources of bodily pleasure in the form of hallucinogenic drugs, brain implants, full-body virtual reality, artificial limbs, replacement organs, etc. Since it is the rich who have access to the best products, class antagonism is reinforced. Cyberpunk generally focuses on the day-to-day "high tech/low life"[1] dichotomy, often depicted by the poorest members of society, especially "punks," embodied by the Capsules in *Akira*. All of this obviously implies deep reflection about the human condition, something cyberpunk has never shied away from. Nevertheless, cyberpunk works aren't required to tackle all of the above. For instance, *Akira* doesn't address the issues of an all-powerful corporation or virtual reality. Subject matters tend to evolve in keeping with the times and the author's vision.

---

1. Advanced technology/poor living conditions.

It makes sense that the first concrete manifestations of cyberpunk in the 1980s appeared in the richest countries of the world. Japan was then at the height of its "economic miracle." And while the archipelago contributed to the birth of the genre, it wasn't just a question of wealth. One must also look at how cyberpunk dominated the markets. The Japanese economic miracle would not have been possible without real innovation in the consumer electronics, robotics, automotive, and communications sectors. Knowing this makes it easier to understand what William Gibson was getting at in a 2001 *Times* article about Japan and cyberpunk: "In the '80s, when I became known for a subgenre of science fiction that journalists called cyberpunk, Japan was already, somehow, the de facto spiritual home of that influence, that particular flavor of popular culture. It was not that there was a cyberpunk movement in Japan or a native literature akin to cyberpunk, but rather that modern Japan simply was cyberpunk. And the Japanese themselves knew it and delighted in it. I remember my first glimpse of Shibuya, after one of the young Tokyo journalists had taken me there. With his face drenched in the light of a thousand media-suns—all that towering, animated crawl of commercial information—he said: 'You see? You see? It is *Blade Runner* town.' And it was. It so obviously was."[2]

"Obviously," that was the adjective that Gibson used. It was as if the evolution toward a cyberpunk landscape was natural for Japan, the inevitable conclusion of its radical transformation into an economic superpower. This is why Gibson set his novel *Neuromancer* in the Chiba Prefecture, despite being unable to place it on a map. This decision was also the result of a kind of "techno-orientalism" that *Akira* certainly reinforced (albeit unintentionally): the mirage of a Japan that the foreigner fantasized as being... well, perhaps not that very different from Neo-Tokyo. After all, has anyone forgotten that even *Blade Runner* featured a geisha on the city's immense advertising screen? And while the bursting of the economic bubble prevented Tokyo from actually becoming a replica of Neo-Tokyo, it is clear that Gibson was right: Japan served as the natural breeding ground for cyberpunk, as well as its very best setting.

So, was *Akira*'s influence on cyberpunk merely aesthetic? Or does the genre's worldbuilding actually depend on its visual aspect, on those "thousands of media-suns" that Gibson saw during his visit to Shibuya? Is the main narrative substance of cyberpunk its setting and, if so, are the shots of Neo-Tokyo (shown at the beginning of the film) enough to tell the story lurking beneath the cityscape's underbelly? These questions are a matter of opinion.

2. William Gibson. "The Future Perfect." *Time*, 30 Apr. 2001.

The cyberpunk genre is intimately linked to the body, both its potential and its limitations. Cyberpunk has always oscillated between fantasy and nightmare, breaking down conceptual barriers and opening up a field of possibilities thanks to scientific progress. It is about the aspiration to be fully in control of ourselves and our environment and the dangers of megalomania (when we forget that we are "merely human"). In this respect, cyberpunk is a veritable horror fest: when individuals lose control of their bodies, when they ask too much of them or become slaves to their desires, the thirst for progress turns against them and they ultimately pay the price for their transgressions. There are very few cyberpunk characters who have not been punished for trying to redefine what it means to be human.

Among *Akira*'s most memorable imagery is the progressive mutation of Tetsuo (the storyline's common thread), as the teenager becomes a combination of metal and flesh before transforming into a pinkish abomination which, thirty years later, still haunts the minds of the most squeamish. When we think of Tetsuo, we cannot help but remember this simultaneously horrific and pitiable image. While, in our minds eye, we always see Kaneda on his big scarlet red motorcycle, it is equally hard to imagine his rival without his bionic right arm and its amalgamation of muscles and metal.

Because the relationship to the body is essential in cyberpunk, we could easily see *Akira* as an offshoot of the horror genre, i.e. body horror, as this subgenre seems to be the logical link between the two. As its name suggests, body horror focuses on disturbing alterations to the human body. It (literally) creates a more visceral sense of unease than does a chase involving a killer or a visit to a haunted house. Such bodily violations fill us with dread, and Tetsuo will ultimately come to experience this stark terror, after a relatively short time of believing that he could modify his body at will (by creating a new right arm with scrap metal, for example).

The portrayal of a future where technology has invaded the human body, in all its intimacy, is just one of the many nightmares described by cyberpunk. David Cronenberg's films, particularly *Scanners* (1981) and *Videodrome* (1984), are often cited as precursors of the genre. The first focuses mainly on telekinesis and the antagonist's ability to use his thoughts to blow people's heads off (as Tetsuo himself can do). In addition to the iconic scene depicting this "mind blowing" mental power, we vividly recall the villain's final face off with the hero, a telekinetic battle that gradually leads to terrifying bodily changes in both opponents. In the manga *Akira*, we see similar scenes involving the drugged soldiers of the Great Tokyo Empire, whose nascent powers cause their faces to swell until their eyes pop out of their sockets. Graphically speaking, nothing is spared, and this is yet another hallmark of body horror. *Videodrome*, on the other hand, is just as bloody, but it is more about social interference, since it deals with the question of mind control via television. The *Videodrome* program within the film "thrusts" a new hallucination-generating organ into the viewer, but that's only the beginning: this organ, which influences perception, allows its host to bend reality, enabling his visions to surpass the stranglehold of subjective perception. But the hero also becomes the victim of *Videodrome*: his abdomen is transformed into a sort of VCR where cassettes can be inserted to "reprogram" him. When he finally regains power over his mind, he fuses his forearm to a pistol and uses it to commit suicide, not out of desperation, but in order to leave behind "the old flesh." Declaring "long live the new flesh," he shoots himself in the head in the hopes of attaining a higher level of existence.

And this is precisely what Tetsuo does in both the film and manga versions of *Akira*: he abandons the flesh in order to transcend reality. Apart from *Videodrome*'s themes of media dependence and people's evolving relationship with television in the 1980s, David Cronenberg's film has a great deal in common with Katsuhiro Otomo's manga. The themes of humanity's evolution and the transcendence of the flesh are found throughout both works. And in both cases, this transcendence must pass through technology, science, and the interconnection between human beings and the environment they construct. In terms of Japanese cinema, the best cyberpunk film is undoubtedly still Shinya Tsukamoto's cult film *Tetsuo: The Iron Man* (1989), whose protagonist's name is directly inspired by *Akira*. This low-budget film, shot in black and white, is barely one hour long. Set against a backdrop of hypnotic industrial music, it follows a *salaryman* whose flesh gradually transforms into iron. Although the script is weak, the quality of the film's special effects is excellent, making it a unique and extremely disturbing visual experience.

Just as the urban landscapes of the 1980s prompted Japan to appropriate the cyberpunk genre, Japanese culture and its relationship to the body also made the archipelago the natural home for body horror. Unlike the Western world, which has historically insisted on body-mind dualism (associating shame with the pleasures of the flesh), the Japanese have maintained a much easier relationship with the body. And while the consumption of alcohol is forbidden among Chinese and Indian Buddhists, this is not the case for Japanese Buddhists.[3] Similarly, there is no mention of an afterlife separate from the real world. That which is worldly is also divine, since

---

3. Hajime Nakamura. *Ways of Thinking of Eastern Peoples: India, China, Tibet, Japan.* University of Hawaii Press, 1981.

"everything is Buddha." This is also true of both elements and objects, with the Japanese regularly putting the honorific prefix "o" before water (*o-mizu*) and tea (*o-cha*). In other words, for most Japanese Shinto and Buddhist sects, the phenomenal world is absolute. There is no question of separating oneself from it or hoping to achieve a purer "existence" through the work of the mind. Culturally speaking, this means that the mind (or soul) is not superior to the body. Sexual desires and drunkenness are not considered shameful, nor are natural bodily functions seen as moral weaknesses. Popular folklore abounds with stories that are in poor taste (at least to the Western mind), with such tales dating back to at least the 11th century. A scroll portraying a terrible battle between flatulists—who use gigantic fans to blow their gas toward their enemies—has been attributed to the painter and abbot (yes, abbot, you read that right) Toba Sojo (1053-1140), also known as Kakuyu![4]

And given that the body and its representations are intimately linked to sex, several major movements in Japanese art and literature attest to a distinctive ease in exploring the flesh, its mysteries, and associated taboos. Let's start by traveling four centuries back in time to Edo (present-day Tokyo). In 1617, the shogunate restricted prostitution in the capital to the district of Yoshiwara, i.e. the "Plain of Happiness." For at least two centuries, Yoshiwara served as the red-light district for those of all classes (with the samurai being among the best clients, even though they were strongly advised to stay away). And yet, it was also considered one of the greatest artistic centers of the time. This was essentially the birthplace of *ukiyo*, or the "floating world" culture, described in a massive body of literature portraying erotic courtesans and amorous play, the latter being (like all things in Japan) highly ritualized. It was also in Yoshiwara that the famous *ukiyo-e* genre developed, and the cultural impact of these woodblock prints resonated far beyond Japan's borders, finding enthusiasts as far away as Europe. *Bijin-ga* (i.e. beautiful women) were one of the major subjects of *ukiyo-e* art. These prints portrayed the red-light district courtesans, but what is of greater interest to us here is of a cruder register, officially forbidden by the authorities: the *shunga*. The latter term literally means "spring pictures" and is a reference to the mating season. The sexual acts depicted in *shunga* prints were not only extremely explicit, they were oftentimes highly exaggerated, especially in terms of genitalia size and positional eccentricity. In 1814, the renowned Katsushika Hokusai (1760-1849) made his most celebrated *shunga* print. Entitled *The Dream of the Fisherman's Wife*, it portrays a naked woman

---

4. Jean-Marie Bouissou. *Manga – Histoire et Univers de la Bande Dessinée Japonaise*. Picquier Poche, 2010.

engaging in sexual intercourse with two octopuses. Two centuries later, the genre's influence on Japanese pornographic production remains clear, as similar imagery is commonplace.

In the late Edo period (the end of the 19th century), another more obscure subgenre of *ukiyo-e* appeared, that of *muzan-e* or "cruel pictures." This artwork emphasized violence and sadism, depicting bloody, sordid, or rape-like murders, with the same eccentricity that tended to push these portrayals beyond the limits of the possible or the sustainable. This subgenre is the precursor of *ero guro* (sometimes referred to as *ero guro nansensu*, the latter meaning nonsense). First appearing in the 1930s, this style mixes eroticism and horror, and its spiritual "muse" is undoubtedly the famous Sada Abe, who killed her lover in 1936 before castrating him with a kitchen knife. [5] The *ero guro* style itself has been echoed by an entire generation of contemporary manga artists, with Suehiro Maruo being its best representative. The Marquis de Sade seems nun-like compared to Maruo, who pushes the limits of decency in all of his works.

The Japanese collective unconscious also remains traumatized by the radioactive fallout effects of the atomic bombs dropped on Hiroshima and Nagasaki. These historical scars are addressed in films like *The H-Man*, as we have mentioned in a previous chapter. A more recent example is the much more voyeuristic *Guinea Pig* series, whose six main episodes were released in Japan between 1985 and 1990. Two of these were directed by the manga artist Hideshi Hino (whom we spoke of earlier, referring to his terrifying *Panorama of Hell*, which retraces the author and his family's flight from Manchuria back to Japan). Halfway between the fake snuff and porn torture genres, these half dozen films essentially consist of long dismemberment scenes featuring even less of a storyline than those put forth in porn movies. Like the director of *Cannibal Holocaust* (1980), Hino was asked to prove that the images of dismemberment were fake, after actor Charlie Sheen, who came across a VHS of the second film, contacted the FBI thinking he had a snuff movie in his possession. Finally, as far as animation is concerned, the best example of the *ero guro* genre is undoubtedly the *Chojin Densetsu Urotsukidoji* OVAs (which appeared between 1987 and 2002). Based on Toshio Maeda's manga series (also known as *Urotsukidoji: Legend of the Overfiend*), they combine tentacle rapes, ultraviolence, sadomasochism, giant monsters, and apocalyptic prophecies. Much more subtle and intelligent than its profligacy would lead us to believe, *Chojin Densetsu Urotsukidoji* demonstrates that the extreme exploration of the body doesn't

5. This was the subject of Nagisa Oshima's highly controversial film *In the Realm of the Senses*, released in 1976.

have to be a simple-minded voyeuristic pleasure, at least not if one can maintain an open mind.

However, in terms of Japanese animation, metamorphosis is not limited to horror films: the *shonen* themselves abound with such cases. Consider Frieza and Cell's transformations in *Dragon Ball Z*, scenes that are not to everyone's taste given that the creatures writhe in pain as their muscles grow, their bones stretch, and their limbs regenerate. Similarly, Togura's metamorphosis in *Yu Yu Hakusho* looks every bit as painful and harrowing, with the human-looking demon doubling in size and tripling in diameter to become an abomination that no longer resembles a man. These sequences, often lasting several minutes, are both visually and auditorily disturbing. The sounds of flesh contorting over growing and/or breaking bones serves as a macabre soundtrack.

The body, sex, and gore. Because Japan is comfortable with carnal experimentation and eccentricity of representation, Japanese cyberpunk was largely characterized by outbursts of violence and body horror between the mid-eighties and mid-nineties, even if it sometimes appeared behind a cute and colorful pop varnish. The video market was in full bloom during this same period, with many studios looking to produce animes that moved beyond the constraints of television: this was the beginning of the OVA market. And it was this new medium that logically produced the bulk of Japanese cyberpunk animation and, with it, a debauchery of violence as excessive and graphic as the images depicted in *muzan-e* or *ero guro*. *Bubblegum Crisis* (1987-1988) and its sequel *Bubblegum Crash*[6] (1991) are textbook examples. In them, we find a number of Japanese animation clichés, including a heroine performing on stage when she's not fighting crime (each of the original series' eight episodes has its own soundtrack, available for purchase). They also feature *tokusatsu* combat armor, hair of all colors, and very typical Japanese humor. And yet, the series doesn't shy away from bloodshed or bodies tearing apart to reveal robotic limbs, and its Tokyo looks a lot like that of *Akira*, at least visually. Deliberately more gory, *Genocyber* (1993) also addresses the subject of metamorphosis and scientists' obsession with the transcendence of the body and the evolution of humanity. In this work, however, the evolution in question clearly results in the creation of a monstrous beast (rather than the shedding of old flesh). The third episode of this series includes a scene that is quite reminiscent of *Akira*. In it, a secret cyborg weapon takes possession of

6. These names were prophetic, given that their creator, Toshimichi Suzuki, associated the word "Bubblegum" with a bubble that could pop at any time. The last OVA had just been released when the Japanese economic bubble burst.

an aircraft carrier, gradually assimilating it in order to turn itself into a biomechanical monster. In a later chapter of Katsuhiro Otomo's manga, Tetsuo (who gradually loses control of his power) also transmutes inert matter into flesh and integrates it into his physical form, an ability that he will use to sink the international fleet that has dared to venture near Neo-Tokyo.

There is no longer much anime like *Bubblegum Crisis* being produced nowadays, as its popularity declined in the years following its release. Starting in the mid-1990s, the tone of Japanese cyberpunk changed, with a greater emphasis placed on the genre's philosophical dimension. This break was probably best exemplified by Mamoru Oshii's 1995 cinematic adaptation of *Ghost in the Shell*, based on Masamune Shirow's manga of the same name. The film's success led to a string of sequels on the both the big and small screen (with *Ghost in the Shell 2: Innocence* garnering mixed reviews due to its overuse of philosophical references). There was even an American live film adaption that came out in 2017. While the Japanese cyberpunk productions of the early eighties and early nineties often had a light-hearted tone and plots that featured high-flying action scenes conducive to the sale of action figures (*Megazone 23*, *Bubblegum Crisis*, *Cyber City Oedo 808*, etc.), they came to espouse the crisis of meaning that had taken over Japan after the bursting of the economic bubble. The genre moved from the "media suns" of *Akira* and *Bubblegum Crisis* to the opaque darkness of *Texhnolyze* (2003), *Ergo Proxy* (2006), and *Serial Experiments Lain* (1998), the latter already prophetically portraying a virtual reality made possible by development of the Internet and new communication networks.

We've been referencing technology quite a bit, but what about medical science? As a fundamental work of the cyberpunk genre, science has a very important place in *Akira*. Science is the breeding ground and raw material from which its humanistic themes emerge. We have already discussed an entire constellation of subjects revolving around misapplied science—such as the radioactive fallout from the atomic bomb—in the first chapter of this book. But *Akira* turns the subject of the atomic disaster on its head by cushioning it. The destruction of Tokyo in Otomo's work is not caused by a bomb, but by an experiment gone wrong. In other words, it is human error that brings about the catastrophic turn of events. As our earlier analysis of *Godzilla* has demonstrated, it is not science itself that is evil. Its proper conduct can remedy even the worst mistakes of humankind.

The backstory of Akira's "creation" (which includes the experimentation he underwent) is the same in both the manga and the film, even if the former does provide more details. Lady Miyako recounts that a handful of scientists at the National Defense Agency collected data about people with unique abilities in the 1960s. Their theories were put into practice when an unnamed controversial figure, specializing in the nervous system, used the results of this research to conduct experiments on living subjects. Ethical conduct was sacrificed in the name of results, so much so that the tests were carried out primarily on children, who were quicker to develop telekinetic abilities without going mad or dying. Many died anyway, but the experiments continued. And then came test subject number 28, also known as Akira, opening up a hopelessly destructive Pandora's box. The secret of Akira is so well kept that even Neo-Tokyo's politicians are not sure whether he is real or a myth. Lady Miyako herself confesses that she doesn't know if the Akira project was entirely supervised by the army or if it was clandestine. But, regardless of the details, we are talking about children being used as guinea pigs. We are speaking of the dehumanization of human beings whose innocence has been sacrificed on the altar of progress. Fiction, of course, is full of megalomaniacal mad scientists. It is the ordinary appearance of the adults, who have turned the children into laboratory rats, that is truly terrifying in *Akira*. In the film version, there is a brief scene showing something akin to affection on the faces of the scientists as they interact with their little human guinea pigs. This is suggestive of either incredible cynicism or the banality of evil.

In either case, the scientists have lost touch with fundamental morality. Isn't this what drives Dr. Moreau, in H.G. Wells novel *The Island of Doctor Moreau* (1896), to isolate himself while carrying out his dreadful experiments? Both in history and fiction, the most radical of scientists have tried to rid themselves of "earthly" considerations (such as the fate of children) in an attempt to access some higher plane. And in doing so, they are, quite simply, "playing god." How many have sought to transcend human existence, and how many more have been determined to be the architects of this transcendence? Kids being experimented on? Collateral damage, a necessary evil. They're simply martyrs of the revolution.

The brutal acceleration of technological progress in the last decades of the 20th century has, of course, breathed new life into science fiction. Because cyberpunk was born in the eighties, the genre sought to imagine the new relationships that might emerge from this progress, with an emphasis on technology, consciousness, and one's relationship to the body. Yesterday's alchemists, who sought immortality in their philosophers' stone, now seek the eternity of the soul, be it via the nervous system or cyberspace. Or both! The conquest of space as a theme, which was quite popular in the animation of the 1970s (with *Space Battleship Yamato*, *Galaxy Express 999*,

Space Pirate Captain Harlock, Mobile Suit Gundam, etc.), gradually dwindled as the genre began to focus more on human beings themselves. From the infinity of the cosmos, we moved to the infinity of the mind.

For those who are even amateur history buffs—and who do not shy away from the truly ugly—the idea of secret experiments carried out on human subjects is hardly inconceivable. Humankind has often been responsible for atrocities that are difficult to accept. Japan is no stranger to this, and it was only thirty some years ago that the absolute horror of one of the best-kept secrets of WWII was uncovered (the "secret of secrets" according to its chief architect), namely the heinous experiments conducted by Unit 731. Headed by General Shiro Ishii, this secret bacteriological research unit disguised itself behind "epidemic prevention" and "water purification" activities to covertly experiment on human beings, with the aim of creating offensive bacteriological weapons.

Many parallels can be drawn between Unit 731 and *Akira*'s scientific division, which used children as guinea pigs. In both cases, the total disregard for human life is evident. General Ishii was well aware of the potential political, public, and diplomatic repercussions of his project, and it was for this reason that he left Japan, moving to occupied Manchuria, in 1932. At the time, Japan (like the United States) had not yet ratified the Geneva Protocol prohibiting the use of chemical and bacteriological weapons,[7] and even if it had, there is no guarantee that a madman like Ishii would have respected international law. The unit ultimately moved to Pingfang, where it carried out the majority of its experiments. It is estimated that approximately 3,000 people lost their lives there, in conditions worthy of the worst horror films. All in all, approximately 10,000 to 12,000 people are thought to have died as a result of Japanese experiments on human beings that began as early as 1932. The effects of various diseases were tested on them, sometimes even going as far as to conduct "live vivisection" on them. They referred to these wretched subjects as *maruta*, which literally means "logs."[8] And because such horror tends to go hand in hand with a certain kind of cynicism, those who were subjected to tests involving flame throwers and other ballistic weapons were dubbed "chopping wood." The unit's printer, Naoji Uezono, who witnessed some of these experiments, later admitted that the human subjects were considered "lumps of meat on a chopping block." It was also discovered that there

7. A minor detail, considering that the Germans bombarded the Allies with chlorine, phosgene, and mustard gas throughout WWI and did so despite having signed the Hague Convention Agreements of 1899 and 1907 (prohibiting the use of such agents).
8. Like the Nazi concentration camp prisoners, they were also assigned a number.

were experiments of even greater questionable utility, such as the surgical joining of body parts. But hey, if it's for science, why bemoan the loss of a few "pieces of meat?"

Regret came much later, although it was far from being unanimously felt. Ishii's authority was absolute. Not only were pre-war Japanese hierarchical structures extremely strict, but his overweening ambitions made him truly untouchable. He was referred to as "Ishii the Honorable" and even "Ishii, God of War." His ambition meant that, at the peak of Unit 731's production, the group had enough germs and bacteria stockpiled to wipe out all of humankind. Not just once, mind you, but several times over.

Because the status of doctors in the Japanese army was far below that of infantry, this was also an opportunity for Ishii to rebalance military hierarchy roles. The twentieth century was an era of scientific progress that would change the face of the world, and the physiognomy of armed conflict was clearly part of it. Atomic, chemical, and bacteriological technologies changed warfare entirely, inevitably luring humankind closer to its own annihilation. But to figures like Ishii, this was of little importance. Referring to the Pacific theater, the imperial propaganda machine spoke of a "holy war" and a Japan whose manifest destiny was to dominate the world.

Akira was published at a time when the latent conflict between the United States and the Soviet Union still elicited fears of nuclear warfare. In 1983, a year after the first chapter of *Akira* was published, American television stations broadcast the TV movie *The Day After* directed by Nicholas Meyer. This anticipatory fiction features several characters before, during, and after a nuclear attack. Remembering where US-Soviet relations were at that point, this "what if" scenario was not so unimaginable. Nearly 100 million television viewers tuned in, and it is even said to have influenced President Ronald Reagan, as it reportedly left him "greatly depressed." While it is difficult to measure the real impact of the film on people's attitudes, its audience success, unparalleled for such a production, is indicative of the American public's fascination with—and terror of—a similarly catastrophic scenario.

Another common point between *Akira* and Unit 731 is the covert nature of scientific activities carried out by the military. Rather surprisingly, politicians are not depicted as megalomaniacal tyrants in Katsuhiro Otomo's work. Instead, they are people who are totally out of touch with reality, people who weren't informed about Akira. This perhaps reflects Japanese history: thirty years earlier, the military had become a "state within the state," distancing itself from the traditional political sphere due to its abandonment of scientific ethics. As mentioned above, General Shiro Ishii intentionally left Japan in order to carry out his experiments, and the chain of command linking him to army commanders remains nebulous even today. In absolute terms, names have been revealed, and the imperial seal has been found on a number of documents. It nevertheless remains difficult to determine who knew what (and to what extent). The policy of total denial—ascribed to by all Ishii's men in the aftermath of Japan's surrender—coupled with the destruction of their precious reports, notes, and documents cast doubts about each individual's responsibility, with the emperor at the top of the list. Only one book really delved into the history of Unit 731 and is still regarded as the ultimate reference: Peter Williams and David Wallace's *Unit 731, Japan's Secret Biological Warfare in World War II.* It is a must read for those who are not faint of heart.

In *Akira* (both the manga and the film), Colonel Shikishima goes to check on the state of the titular character's cryogenic prison. While doing so, he references a similar race to destroy evidence. The colonel doesn't even try to disguise his shame over the actions of his predecessors: "What a disgrace! Look how much of a hurry they were in when they built this place...They were afraid... Ashamed... They chose to conceal it by burying the roots of a great civilization... Turned their backs on what science had to offer them... And tried to seal away forever the hole they had torn open with their own hands." Besides anger and disgust, Shikishima's words also suggest a certain regret, a longing for the scientific advances that military research could have made before it went off the rails. Before becoming an ultra-nationalist psychopath, General Ishii was a brilliant mind. He had been known to put his intelligence to use for the common good. He was credited with the invention of a revolutionary motorized water filter that saved the lives of many soldiers, preventing them from contracting cholera from dirty drinking water. This feat elevated the entire army medical corps by putting them ahead of the commissariat and the engineers, who until then were the exclusive providers of pure water during military campaigns. But the fictional Shikishima issues a telling caveat concerning "advancement": "Keep your feet on the ground! I can't risk millions of lives... Just to satisfy your "scientific curiosity"... And your ego!" In the end, Ishii was not arrested, but granted immunity by the United States in exchange for his scientific knowledge. It is even strongly suspected that the results of Ishii's experiments are what allowed the Americans to use bacteriological weapons during the Korean War...

Science is first and foremost a human discipline. The hand that directs it is what determines whether it is beneficial or harmful. *Akira* is far from being the only manga to portray scientists who get caught up in their research, but not all "bad" scientists are megalomaniacs by nature. Humankind is weak, and our fallibility is often the cause of wrongdoing.

We thus hate the Doctor in *Hellsing* while pitying Shou Tucker in *Fullmetal Alchemist*, even though both are guilty of unbelievable atrocities. And who knows, perhaps *Akira*'s scientists weren't all monsters... Could some have taken on the project without knowing its full scope? Several members of Unit 731 expressed their regrets after the experiments came to a halt, claiming that they were simply "following orders." On what scale do we measure evil, especially when someone is barely twenty years old?

Earlier, we mentioned the importance of youth in post-war Japanese fiction, particularly in manga and animation. This generational divide holds adults accountable for their past mistakes. It also empowers children to rectify them and lead the way to a better tomorrow. *Akira* maintains this split by highlighting the destructive actions of the older generation. As test subjects, the children were robbed of the most beautiful period of their lives. Their premature aging coupled with their lack of growth makes them definitively unique. Unaffected by time, they become anomalies whose very appearance is senseless. They have been stripped of their names in exchange for a number, just like the prisoners in the Nazi concentration camps. Scientists have constructed a dreamlike fantasy world for them, but in the end, it is nothing but a sham. Kiyoko sleeps in a princess bed as if she's awaiting a kiss from Prince Charming, while her only visitors are men wearing white coats or military fatigues. The discrepancy between the horror of the children's elderly appearance and their cute toys, dolls, and stuffed animals is also highlighted by their nightmarish visions, which are projected onto these objects. In addition, the children's propensity to develop their "powers" can be read as a tribute to their sacrosanct innocence, an innocence that the adults are wrong to exploit. Childhood is not a time for rational explanations: it is a time for magic. As for Tetsuo, he becomes overwhelmed because he is no longer a passive, naive child. The violent complexity of his emerging adult personality has changed everything.

THE IMPACT OF
AKIRA

A MANGA
[R]EVOLUTION

2.5: Creature: Tetsuo
(Second Phase)

TETSUO'S PUNY PHYSIQUE sits astride the former gang kingpin's giant motorcycle as he leads the procession of Clowns. Everyone is intimidated by the young man, adding to his sense of invulnerability. This is somewhat understandable, given that he can blow his enemies' heads off with a simple twitch of the eyebrows. Nonetheless, there is strength in numbers, and this adage is at the heart of the *bosozoku*'s codes. By defying their principles, Tetsuo has also rejected this group logic, a rationale that has protected him ever since he first joined the Capsules. And because he believes that he is impervious to danger, Tetsuo has no idea that he's about to walk into a trap. Yamagata has called upon several Capsule gang members, and they are planning to ambush their former sidekick in an old warehouse... But Tetsuo is no longer the timid teenager they once knew, and their plan fails miserably. The young man emerges from the scuffle unscathed. He finds himself facing Kaneda, who intends to make him pay for his latest transgressions. During the ensuing standoff, Tetsuo once again accuses his former friend of being a long-standing tyrant, to which Kaneda derisively responds: "I hear you're running something now, too... A cesspool."

Kaneda's words do not go over well. This is hardly surprising: Tetsuo's rebellion was triggered by a perceived lack of mutual respect. Having seen what their former comrade is capable of, Yamagata implores Kaneda to shoot, but the Capsule leader is torn. This amuses Tetsuo, who begins toying with his prey. It is Yamagata who finally takes aim, pointing a gun at his former pal. But his head explodes before he has time to pull the trigger.[1] Kaneda then retrieves the weapon and, in a fit of rage, shoots Tetsuo.

Seeing the blood bloom from his abdomen, the latter immediately loses his bravado. Having believed that he was a god, Tetsuo is now in danger of slowly bleeding out. To make matters worse, the migraine that has been troubling him for days is now unbearable. Hoping for some relief, the young man is ready to throw himself into the arms of the newly arrived soldiers, however childish this might seem. Surprisingly, Tetsuo quickly recovers by swallowing a powerful drug, restoring both his equilibrium and his hubris. Colonel Shikishima then convinces Tetsuo to accompany him, both to be

---

1. Yamagata dies in a similar manner in the film, but much later in the chronology.

stabilized and to better learn how to master his powers. The military man is well aware that the teenager is at an impasse. As dangerous as Tetsuo has proven to be, he is currently unable to survive without a constant supply of drugs, a state of affairs that he is still struggling to accept. He is tottering on the edge of a precipice, one that he tries to ignore throughout the entire manga.

While the Capsules consume second-rate pills for purely recreational purposes, this is not the case for Tetsuo. His reliance on psychotropic drugs quickly becomes a living nightmare. This is not simply the anguish of an addict who pops pills like throat lozenges and sees his supply dwindling. The drugs that Tetsuo relies upon have a symbolic value: they are a continual reminder of the very neuroticism he is trying to escape by swallowing the capsules in the first place. It's a vicious and never-ending cycle.

Many symbols come to mind when we mention *Akira*: most notably Kaneda's motorcycle, the exchanges "Tetsuoooo" and "Kanedaaaa" which have become memes over time, and Tetsuo's terrifying transformation into a mass of pink flesh. But *Akira* also evokes the image of a 1986 Otomo art logo featuring a red and blue capsule. This logo appears on the back of Kaneda's jacket along with the words: "*Good for health, bad for education.*" The jacket's design was specifically chosen for the film. Viewers see it in the scene introducing Kaneda, who conveniently has his back turned toward the camera as he fiddles with the Harukiya bar jukebox. This symbol, composed of a simple yet striking color combination, enables outsiders to quickly identify Kaneda and his gang.

They are thus unofficially dubbed the "Capsules" and henceforth associated with the aforementioned red and blue logo. Simultaneously addicted to and repulsed by the drug that keeps him "stabilized," Tetsuo naturally associates it with his former friends. This does not make things any easier for him psychologically. Tetsuo's inability to control his growing power can be interpreted as the brutal reemergence of the inferiority complex that he tries to suppress through violence and his status as the new king of a "cesspool." When his unconscious impulses caution him to remain humble and avoid overestimating himself, Tetsuo turns his back on reason and silences the nagging voices by stuffing himself full of capsules. But doesn't this just remind him of the impossibility of escaping his neuroses? The only way for Tetsuo to find peace of mind is to recognize and accept his addiction to "Capsules" (both the bikers and the drugs) and thus swallow his ego, rather than trying to compensate by putting on airs. His posturing is a form of self-deception: the respite that it offers is just a temporary fix for a nightmare that continues to grow increasingly darker. Essentially, his ego is his dealer.

Once the army takes him into custody, Tetsuo reads the minds of his hosts-cum-jailers. This leads him to the prematurely aged children and his ensuing fight with them in the nursery. The young man has been obsessed with the idea of meeting Akira ever since he first heard the latter's name. He intends to reawaken him. Colonel Shikishima tries to convince him to abandon this dangerous plan, but it is too late. In the manga, Tetsuo proves that he can no longer be controlled by Shikishima. He knocks the colonel to the ground and then subdues him by placing his foot on the man's skull: "Think you're so tough... Big guy like you..." Kaneda shows up just in the nick of time, and the two rivals engage in a brief fight, forcing Tetsuo to flee. In the film, the two young men exchange a few words, the meaning of which is particularly important in the original Japanese version. Tetsuo calls Kaneda "Kane-*chan*." The suffix -*chan* is generally reserved for small children, animals, or anything that is considered "cute." It therefore has a diminutive connotation in more serious speech, and to address a superior using the suffix -*chan* is extremely indelicate at best and a provocation at worst.

This brings us back to our discussion of the *bosozoku* hierarchy in previous chapters. Tetsuo addresses Kaneda in this manner whenever he gets the upper hand in a fight. Toward the end of the film, after yet another provocation, Kaneda retorts: "Use-*san!*" This is the most common (gender-neutral) suffix in the Japanese language. There is yet another Japanese subtlety that we should mention. In Japan, seniority takes precedence over merit, meaning that no matter what your role is, you will always address someone who has been around longer than you, or who has once been your superior, as well ... a superior. Always. The anthropologist Chie Nakane provides a clear explanation of this custom in his book *Japanese Society*: "Let us imagine, for example, the case of X, once a student of Y, who, fifteen years afterward, becomes a professor in the same department as Y and thus acquires equal status. X still addresses Y as *sensei* and will not refer to him as *doryo* (colleague) to a third person. Y may address X as *kun*, treating him, as a *kohai*,[2] even in front of X's students or outsiders: Y has to be most broad-minded and sociable to address X as *sensei* in such a context."[3]

In the manga, Tetsuo manages to free Akira from his cryogenic prison but, as soon as he does so, shots from the Satellite Orbital Laser pulverize his arm and the young man is forced to abandon the little boy. Tetsuo

---

2. *Kohai* refers to someone with less experience than a *senpai*, in this case X as compared to Y.
3. Chie Nakane. *La Société Japonaise*. Armand Colin, 1974 (1970 for the English version).

then disappears for most of the third volume (of the six *tankobon*), only to resurface after Akira wipes out Neo-Tokyo. This will mark the beginning of Tetsuo's new reign, as he will go from being the king of a cesspool to the ruler of a ruined city.

THE IMPACT OF
AKIRA

A MANGA
[R]EVOLUTION

2.6: Creature: Catastrophe
& Reconstruction

HE MAJOR DIFFERENCE between the manga and the animated film version of *Akira* is the lack of a major narrative arc in the latter, namely the second cataclysm brought about by Akira, and the new balance of power that arises in the ruinous cityscape of Neo-Tokyo. The manga thus abandons its portrayal of a cyberpunk dystopia and turns toward post-apocalyptic fiction, moving from the urban effervescence of *Blade Runner* to the scrap metal desert of *Mad Max*. The story's cut-off point occurs when Tetsuo goes off to find Akira. In the film, the little boy has been dead for a long time, thus eliminating a number of plot lines that the manga had developed over time. The "Great Tokyo Empire" narrative arc is thus completely abandoned, with the film's conclusion becoming a simplified version of the one that readers would discover two years later, in 1990, when the last chapter of the manga was published.

A brief recap is in order, especially for those who never read the manga. Akira, who is alive and well, becomes the target of various groups, including the military, the revolutionaries, and the private army serving the shady career politician named Nezu. When he sees his friend Takashi get killed by a stray bullet, Akira, who hadn't yet made a peep, becomes furious and wipes out much of Neo-Tokyo, just as he destroyed the previous city in 1982. A few days later, the rubble of the once luminous city becomes a giant hunting ground for looters, and the tenet that "might makes right" naturally prevails. Alongside the independent gangs (marauders on the lookout for both food and females), two large factions form and ultimately vie for the control of Neo-Tokyo. On the one side is the Great Tokyo Empire, with Akira acting as its figurehead emperor. Tetsuo serves as the government's so-called prime minister and spokesman and is assisted by an unnamed character who nevertheless plays an important role in the manga. Unlike the rest of the survivors, this aide is always well dressed. He is basically an opportunist who oversees the activities, gatherings, rituals, and military campaigns of the newly formed Empire. On the other side is the enigmatic Lady Miyako, who assists the tired, the poor, and the hungry. Not only does she take in those who are sick and wounded, she also teaches her long-time followers how to master their telekinetic powers. A victim of army experimentation herself, her hand has been branded with the number 19. She belongs to the generation of test subjects that preceded Akira's and is now the sole survivor of these "preliminary" tests.

Catastrophic scenarios resonate with the Japanese. After having faced atomic annihilation, not once, but twice, the archipelago is regularly inundated by natural disasters. The most recent dates back to the 2011 earthquake that precipitated a terrible tsunami and the ensuing Fukushima Daini Nuclear Power Plant disaster. Perhaps more than any other populace, the Japanese are aware of the potential for an abrupt, inevitable end. Their sword of Damocles is referred to as the "Big One," a major earthquake that is expected to hit Japan in the next few years. The entire country is trying to prepare accordingly. And yet, Japan has always risen up to rebuild that which was destroyed, as evidenced by the Kanto (1923), Kobe (1995), and Tohoku (2011) earthquakes. This culture of catastrophe, of imminent annihilation, thus goes hand in hand with a culture of rebirth, an heir, at least in part, to the Buddhists' belief in resurrection cycles and their understanding of impermanence. In fact, the Ise Grand Shrine, in the prefecture of Mie, has been deliberately demolished and rebuilt every twenty years for thirteen centuries, symbolizing this perpetual rebirth via a reconstruction that takes on the appearance of a popular ritual.

Whether or not Otomo's Neo-Tokyo will be rebuilt with such fervor remains uncertain. Its annihilation has resulted in the destruction of the collective superego, the inhabitants' internalization of cultural rules. The illusory luxury, comfort, and prosperity that once reigned in Neo-Tokyo are now distant memories. The survivors' base instincts have been awakened, perhaps for the very first time. And while violence existed in the city long before it toppled like a house of cards, it now becomes rawer, dirtier. We witness scenes that are difficult to bear, especially in the case of Kei who, on several occasions, finds herself pursued by gangs of young men who try to rape her. Like life itself, dignity no longer has much value in post-disaster Neo-Tokyo. When the urge to consume is no longer satisfied by goods or services, individuals who are slaves to their impulses seek that which is available to them. Morality goes out the window. And since rape is primarily about power, physical and sexual domination responds to a primitive logic: the law of the jungle, especially in a new world where social hierarchies have yet to be established. When savages plunder a village, they do not rape the women because they are sex obsessed. They do so to assert their superiority through brute force and violence, belittling and denying the very humanity of those they have defeated.

Since the people have been dispossessed of their dignity, along with everything else, the emergence of a new society must be accompanied by a new search for meaning. The old gods are dead. Money is now worthless. Neo-Tokyo must therefore go through a period of reconstruction involving the constitution of a new mythology and the establishment of new idols. The saintly figure of Lady Miyako and the messianic figure of Akira are naturally venerated to meet the populace's unconscious desire for divine protection. This is because the desperate masses are indeed looking for a strong symbolic figure to hold onto, whether it be the protective Lady Miyako or the conquering Akira. Neo-Tokyo's survivors submit to these two god-like authority figures, like children seeking parental guidance. In their own way, both Lady Miyako and Akira relieve them of the burden of uncertainty. Miyako even mentions this to Tetsuo, when he comes to her seeking answers: "Man is woefully shortsighted. He huddles upon the ground, staring down at his own feet. It is only when he is afraid that he considers the other world, and then he will gladly sell his soul to whatever God or Buddha offers him hope." Jerome Shapiro, the author of the intriguing book *Atomic Bomb Cinema: The Apocalyptic Imagination on Film*, tends to agree, explaining that: "The first responsibility of any community or any leader that's experiencing a catastrophic event is finding hope. Without hope there is no change. When you look at the scholarship on ancient apocalyptic literature, rather than, say the nuclear crisis we're experiencing today, what we find is that so and so agrees that this is a hopeful literature. Yet it describes painful events that will come, it describes suffering and oppression that is taking place. They're saying that if we get through this, there's a possibility of rebuilding communities, finding greater meaning in life, and finding happiness... The first responsibility of any literature is to encourage people to survive and self-actualize in themselves, and then only is the possibility of restoring community possible... In the Japanese tradition, the world comes to a complete end and another starts anew."[1]

This quote supports our previous analysis of end-of-the-world scenarios (including those involving an atomic bomb) in both manga and anime, i.e. that total annihilation is always followed by a period of renewal, with people dreaming of something "better" just as they do at the end of *Space Runaway Ideon: Be Invoked*. While a good deal of the universe ends up being annihilated in this series, the characters' souls depart for another world: they have the chance to begin anew. In *Akira*, the army makes use of mobile units capable of sheltering several people at curfew time. Speaking of these mechanical, radiation-insensitive weapons, one soldier says, "Even if everyone dies, the robots will be here to protect the land." To put it simply, there is a kind of eternity in Japanese fiction, one that outlives its inhabitants and perhaps gives rise to new life in a better future world.

1. Jerome Shapiro. Interview by Fred Nielsen. Omaha, Nebraska, 5 Aug. 2002.

The Great Tokyo Empire is charged with a symbolic energy that is resolutely masculine. It is comprised of men, with "recruited" women serving as mere objects of sexual desire. The Empire rapidly becomes militarized, launches an aggressive propaganda campaign, and clearly demonstrates its lust for conquest. While each of its members are proud to be a part of it, the unaffiliated—especially those who oppose it—remain unimpressed. They refer to the Great Empire as a cult, and there is indeed a sectarian logic behind the regime's practices, rituals, beliefs, and communications. Akira's silence reinforces the mystery, and thus the fear, that surrounds him. He indulges in various demonstrations of power that are quickly deemed "miracles," thus attracting an increasing number of "followers." The latter see the child's impassivity as form of divine purity: he is both stolid and untouchable. He is given a makeshift throne and modern emperor's clothing, and his coveted appearances are quite rare. It is thus a great privilege to see the emperor. Meanwhile Tetsuo's aide quickly grasps the mechanics of power and becomes the Empire's main spokesman. By offering the rabble fresh water rations drugged with capsules, a benevolent gift from Akira, he not only satisfies their tired bodies, he also makes them feel closer to the god that they worship. This establishes not only a material dependency, but an emotional and spiritual one as well. Referring to the Japanese social hierarchy and the people's relationship with their leader, Chie Nakane writes that "for weak people the emotional security deriving from the strong leader-follower relationship creates a peaceful world. It is significant that the new religious sects that proliferated after the war based their group organization on an emotional, vertical line, mediating direct contact through a hypnotic leader." [2]

Such faith is reinforced by collectivism: the Great Empire's ritualistic gatherings serve to promote the group's beliefs. When a spy is unmasked, his execution is a public one. He is made a spectacle of, much like the women who were burned at the stake during the Salem Witch Trials. Such a ritual kills several birds with one stone. Not only does it send a powerful message to dissidents, it also reinforces the beliefs, and thus the unity, of the "faithful." The punishment that is meted out is an act of will. Seeing someone burnt at the stake was an opportunity to "appreciate" the newly restored order, to correct an error, to change course. Having survived the catastrophe, Colonel Shikishima witnesses a telling scene. In a drug-induced trance, proponents of the Great Empire take part in an epileptic dance around an impromptu fire. Here, the cult turns to shamanism, the latter being among the most ancient of all spiritual and religious practices.

---

2. Chie Nakane. *La Société Japonaise*. Armand Colin, 1974 (1970 for the English version).

Shamanic trances are intended to diminish individuality, so that the divine can express itself through the vehicle of the body. It's a form of religious ecstasy (*ex-stasis*, "being outside of oneself") whose goal is transcendence, a desire to better understand and experience the universe, the cosmos, or as Miyako says "the flow." Similarly, the Great Tokyo Empire's rally–the one that ends with Tetsuo tearing a massive hole in the Moon's surface– opens with the lighting of the Olympic flame (in an unfinished stadium that will, most likely, never be completed). The Olympic Stadium is yet another symbol of power. But while the architectural marvel constructed for the (real) 1964 Tokyo Olympic Games was a sign of Japan's rebirth and the beginnings of its economic miracle, *Akira*'s stadium barely survived the recent catastrophe and is in danger of collapsing due to its weakened foundation. Like Kaneda said, Tetsuo rules over a cesspool.

The post-apocalyptic world is a fertile breeding ground for the emergence of a basic spirituality, a return to core beliefs. When absolutely everything (buildings, monuments, the social fabric, values, etc.) has been destroyed, the instinctual will to live just isn't enough. To build a civilization, people need a solid, common foundation. This involves a search for meaning, a more or less metaphysical justification for their presence in the here and now. George Miller's *Mad Max* series is full of proto-civilizations born from the ruins of the old, especially in the third film, *Mad Max Beyond Thunderdome* (1985). In it, the wandering protagonist, Max, meets a tribe of children stuck in the middle of nowhere. A bit like the boys in William Golding's *Lord of the Flies* (1954), the young people are the survivors of an airplane crash. The adults, who left to seek help, never returned. Max learns about the tribe's origin at a ritualistic gathering, known as the Tell. An elder named Savannah recounts a fictional version of the story, giving fanciful names to even the most common of objects and phenomena. The airplane becomes a flying raft, turbulence takes on the attributes of a violent gang, illuminated roads turn into rivers of light, etc. Not only does Savannah use cave drawings to illustrate her tale (reminding us of Lascaux), she also employs a bamboo device (whose rectangular form resembles a television screen) to frame the drawings depicting past events. The group possesses a stereoscopic slide-viewer as well. The images it displays are "artifacts" from what they believe is a distant past, i.e. the time before the Pox-eclipse (a play on the word "apocalypse"). The tribe believes that Max is Captain Walker, the pilot who led the group of adults off to seek aid. According to "prophecy," the captain will return to guide the children to their promised land, known in the movie as Tomorrow-Morrow Land. In the end, of course, everything works out, and the children's misfortunes morph into a happy ending. But the underlying meaning is clear: it is the prophecy that gives them hope. This is the tie that binds the group together, and the ritual of the Tell, enlivened by the audience's active participation in the form of mantra-like repetition, uplifts their morale. In a more recent film, *Mad Max: Fury Road*, the tyrannical Immortan Joe rules over an army of faithful servants. These young adults, known as the War Boys (or the Fukushima kami-crazy War Boys)[3] are entirely devoted to his cause. Like the Japanese World War II kamikaze pilots that they are obviously modeled after, the War Boys worship their leader, whose absolution is considered a supreme honor. Their self-sacrifice in battle, symbolized by the motto *"I live, I die, I live again!"* is synonymous with immortality, a ticket to the paradise of warriors, the Valhalla promised by the cult of the V8 engine. The world may be a desert wasteland, but a spark of divinity persists. The people surrender themselves to a new liturgy, and while it may be questionable, it is preferable to total chaos. And despite the shift in tone, Yoshihisa Tagami's science fiction manga *Grey* (1985, adapted into an OVA in 1986)—which takes place in an equally apocalyptic setting—is also chock-full of religious terms and imagery. Among the dilapidated buildings, we see *jinja* (Shinto temples), and the combat robots are referred to as *aum* (Brahman's mantra in Hinduism) or *rama* (a Hindu deity). As for the resistance leaders, they are called *guji* (Shinto priests). The same goes for *Neon Genesis Evangelion*, whose lexicon is decidedly Judeo-Christian. Hideaki Anno has always denied that the series is a reinterpretation of biblical themes, stating that his borrowings were only meant to make it "cool." Nonetheless, the apocalypse takes on a different feel when one mixes in Adam, Lilith, Angels, Dead Sea Scrolls, and the Kabbalah Tree of Life...

We create myths in order to connect with the divine. All civilizations have at least been tempted to do so: after all, aren't myths the equivalent of what we now refer to as a "national narrative?" *South Park* pokes fun at *Mad Max 3* and the Telling in *The M Word Episode* (i.e. The Wacky Molestation Adventure, season 4, episode 16). Left to their own devices, the children are living like savages in a desolate, run-down South Park. Stan explains the origin of this situation to a couple of strangers. In a ritual similar to the Telling, he says that he and his friends came up with a way "to have all the birth-givers disappear by using the magic M word," meaning that they lied about their parents molesting them in order to get rid them. Their divine figure, the "Provider," is a statue of the famous American football player John Elway. At the end of the episode, we learn that the adults have only been gone for ten whole days.

---

3. The film was released in 2015, four years after the Fukushima Daiichi nuclear power plant disaster.

There is a term for the mistaken divinization of objects or activities resulting from culture shock, i.e. "the cargo cult." During WWII, native tribes of the Melanesia islands met Japanese and American soldiers, who arrived with equipment and technology that they had never seen before. Cults and rituals were formed on the basis of imitation. When the soldiers radioed for supplies, the natives saw food and clothing being delivered to them by air. They responded by building fake radios and drop zones so that "providence" would bring them an abundance of riches. Sixty years later, there were still some Vanuatu tribesmen building dummy landing pads and praying in front of their idols (DC-3 transport planes)!

South Park's satire thus reveals an astute insight: those living in misery often long for the intervention of a divine savior. Of course, this universal concept is not limited to post-apocalyptic fiction. Stephen King explores this same psychological weakness in his 1980 novella *The Mist*. In this short horror story, inhabitants of a small town find themselves trapped in a supermarket when a thick mist appears, a mist that seems to give rise to fearsome creatures. Isolation and despair cause the townspeople to relinquish more and more power to a religious zealot named Mrs. Carmony, who claims that these events signal the arrival of Judgment Day. Her announcement of the imminent apocalypse and her calls for atonement appeal to those who are most fearful. It isn't long before the supermarket refugees find themselves divided into two camps: the believers and the heretics. This tension reaches its climax when Mrs. Carmody calls for young Billy (the protagonist's son) to be sacrificed, leading to a violent riot. When the woman is finally shot in the head, the hold that she has on her followers disappears almost immediately. With their spiritual leader dead, the shepherd's flock is lost.

Lady Miyako makes a brief appearance in the film *Akira*. Her small role is radically different than that of her manga counterpart, since she is the head of an apocalyptic cult prophesying about the return of Akira and the end of the world (ironically, this is pretty much what happens). Her alarmist diatribe finds an audience amidst the backdrop of protests spreading throughout Neo-Tokyo like wildfire. In the end, this version of Lady Miyako[4] dies a miserable death when she inadvertently gets caught in the middle of Tetsuo's fight with the army. The appearance of a cult prophesying the end of the world is a classic theme, a common symptom of a crisis of meaning within society itself. It thus comes as little surprise to see eccentric figures with zany beliefs in the cyberpunk universe. After

4. There was some confusion surrounding Miyako in the French and American versions: she was given a man's voice in the dubs!

all, the genre tends to favor sick societies, suffering from overconsumption, extreme pollution, and social chaos (when it isn't addressing the complex subject of transhumanism).

In the mid-nineteenth century, Japan began to see a surge of new religious sects. Rather than offering an understanding of the world and how to arrive at acceptance (as Buddhism and Shintoism tend to do), these movements motivated believers to take actions to improve their lives, their well-being, and sometimes their chance of salvation. They combined elements of Shintoism, Buddhism, Confucianism, and varying degrees of personal development. Since the 1970s and '80s, there has even been talk of "new new religions" (*shin-shinshukyo*), a phenomenon that is often compared to the Western new age movement. [5] Major changes in post-war Japanese society have given rise to a range of (more or less esoteric) movements, which have served as a counterbalance for the members of society who cannot or can no longer find their place in modern Japan. Furthermore, as the year 2000 approached, apocalyptic predictions multiplied around the world, and Japan was no exception. In 1973, Ben Goto published *Nostradamus no Daiyogen* (*Prophecies of Nostradamus*), a work that introduced the famous seer to the Japanese public and met with a certain degree of success. Goto based his book on Nostradamus' premise that the world would end in 1999, but of course this turned out to be just as "true" as the MIR station crashing into Paris. The same year that Goto's book came out, Sakyo Komatsu's best-selling fictional work *Nihon Chinbotsu* (*Japan Sinks*) was released. It describes a catastrophic scenario in which tectonic forces wipe out the Japanese archipelago. Of course, at the time, many manga and anime portrayed similar end-of-the-world scenarios: a natural result of the Pacific Wars, the two atomic bombs, and the post-war climate, all of which were discussed in the first chapter of this section.

The failure of the student movements in the late 1960s certainly played a role in young people's growing adherence to these new religions. As the fanciful narrative of a perpetually successful Japan lost followers, these "alternative" paths met with increasing enthusiasm. But then, on March 20, 1995, the Aum Shinrikyo (Supreme Truth) sect succeeded in carrying out the deadly Tokyo subway sarin attack. This act of domestic terrorism, which deeply shocked Japan, killed thirteen people and wounded hundreds more (fifty of whom were seriously injured). It nevertheless said a lot about the state of Japanese society in the middle of the "lost decade," following the bursting of the economic bubble. Aum Shinrikyo was a doomsday sect that was part of the *shin-shinshukyo* movement, although the term *karuto* (a

---

5. Jean-Pierre Berthon & Naoki Kashio. "Les Nouvelles Voies Spirituelles au Japon : Etats des Lieux et Mutations de la Religiosité." *Archives de Sciences Sociales des Religions*, 2000.

Japanese word meaning cult) has also been frequently used to describe the group. As it became progressively more radical, its founder Shoko Asahara[6] predicted that the world would end around the year 2000. Once again, the writings of Nostradamus were used to support the guru's claim, and it was said that only the most faithful would escape the catastrophe to come, in this case, a US-initiated World War III. This worst-case scenario, coupled with secrecy, enables cults to hold onto their followers. Once such "knowledge" is shared with believers, the latter see it as a divine gift or privilege. They then enter the closed circle of initiates, and any departure from the cult is not only inadvisable, it is synonymous with death. The Aum Shinrikyo sect kidnapped and imprisoned deserters, and there were even instances of poisoning and murder. Discipline within the sect became ridiculously strict over time, as no contact with the outside world was allowed. Asahara even went so far as to banish those with type O blood:[7] they were supposedly "unreliable individuals likely to weaken the Buddha's teachings."[8] Once the sect's activities came to light, the Japanese were horrified by the youthfulness of its members, especially the high-ranking ones. Aum Shinrikyo was primarily made up of young men, under thirty years of age, with solid university backgrounds in chemistry, medicine, law, etc. Their skills were valuable to the sect. We must remember that Japan was in crisis in the mid-1990s. It was the younger generation who ended up paying the highest price for past errors, from the bursting of the economic bubble to the collapse of a model that was believed to be infallible. There was the ever-lessening chance of finding a good job after completing one's university studies, and the sect promised a "group solidarity" that young graduates would have been hard-pressed to find on the job market. In addition, the sect had an extremely well-oiled communications plan to help it attract more members. There were also a few manga and short anime series featuring Asahara, which contributed to an anti-manga wave in the nineties, much like the protests against hard rock and video games following the Columbine High School shooting in April 1999. Incidentally, the sect had devices that they referred to as "Cosmo Cleaners" to thwart poisonous gas attacks, a direct reference to *Space Battleship Yamato* and the technology used to cleanse the Earth's atmosphere.

When the fictional Neo-Tokyo is destroyed, these same "guarantees" of wealth and affluence disappear along with it. The survivors are robbed of

6. Sentenced to death in 2004 (during what the Japanese referred to as the "trial of the century"), he was ultimately executed on July 6, 2018.
7. In Japan, blood type is superstitiously linked to personality, just as astrological signs are in Western countries.
8. Sylvaine Trinh. "Aum Shinrikyô : Secte et Violence." *Culture et Conflits*, no. 29-30, 1998.

the very narrative they bought into, only to be left with broken dreams and the pressing need to rebuild. Miyako and Akira both embody a quick fix, forcing the inhabitants to make a choice. Do they want a reassuring maternal figure to protect them or would they rather follow an enigmatic and powerful leader whose bid for power excites them? This binary opposition essentially polarizes Neo-Tokyo's remaining populace, with the majority of women and children supporting Miyako and the men backing Akira. But in the latter case, the promise of transcendence is just as false as Aum Shinrikyo's "prophecies." The so-called creation of a new Eden is an illusion fueled by the consumption of psychotropic substances. The proffered Promised Land includes no mention of values, a new social contract, or the salvation of the soul. It just glorifies a synthetic, artificial power. And yet, Akira does manage to shy away from power games despite playing the role of divine emperor. He appears to draw some semblance of truth from the capsules themselves: we see the little boy levitating them to form a double DNA-like helix. Because Akira has never been a slave to the ego and its temptations, he is able to tear apart the veil of illusion and see the unspeakable truth that lies just beyond consciousness. In this, he differs from Tetsuo, who has long made the mistake of appreciating his powers for their material strength alone.

It is only in the film version of *Akira* that we truly get a taste of the millenarian sect. This is because Lady Miyako has assumed an entirely different role, as we have previously pointed out. We see her preaching in the streets of Neo-Tokyo on multiple occasions, and her message is much more extreme than the ideas attributed to her in the manga. Believing Akira to be a messiah, who has come to purify Japan of its sins, she tells the populace: "Beware of those who distort providence under the guise of science! Under the guise of development, we find waste after waste! Under the guise of culture, we find desolation of the human heart! It is time to repent for all sins! The time to awake is near! The time of the great Akira's awakening is near!" She is nothing like her benevolent counterpart in the manga. When Tetsuo manages to escape from the army and effort-lessly starts decimating their tanks and helicopters, a troop of the newly "converted" join him, believing that he is the prophesied Akira whom they have been waiting for. Those in the crowd who doubt the new Messiah's identity are shamelessly beaten. The Lady Miyako of the film denounces science and progress, which is rather ironic given that Tetsuo is the result of both. She seems to be advocating a return to a more "primitive" society. Nostalgia for an ancient divinized era is commonplace among the Japanese, as Joseph Kitagawa, an eminent specialist in Asian religions and a pioneer in religious history studies, points out: "Historically, such a yearning of the Japanese people to restore the idealized state of the golden days, coupled with the notion of the unity of religion and politics (*saisei-itchi*), has often developed a messianic fervor, especially during political crises. The ethnocentric, messianic restorationism implicit in the indigenous religious tradition of Japan received further stimulus from the apocalyptic notion of Buddhism known as *mappo* (the coming of the age of degeneration of the Buddha's Law), as well as from the "immanental theocratic" motif of Confucianism."[9] This *mappo* announces the arrival of a new Buddha, in this case the newly "awakened" Akira, and the beginning of a new cycle.

The end of the manga comes as a bit of a surprise, even if it does roughly correspond to that of the film, at least in terms of Tetsuo's fate and Akira's final disappearance. The major difference is the manga's inclusion of the international relief workers, who appear on the periphery of the city and disembark to aid the survivors following the third and final cataclysm. But instead of the anticipated return to peace and a hope-filled epilogue, Kaneda turns on the newcomers, plundering their resources and declaring the birth of the Great Akira Empire. He then kicks the dazed disaster relief forces out of the new empire's "territory".

Why would Kaneda do such a thing? While we'll never know for sure, there seems to be at least two possibilities, and they are not mutually exclusive. On the one hand, there is the definitive rejection of a generation whose mistakes have destroyed the Japanese capital three times over, with this broken trust prompting Kaneda's gang to reject all offers of outside help. And on the other hand, there is the urgency for self-determination, a drive embodied by the Capsules and their leader since the very beginning of the manga. The streets that they take to on their worn-out bikes may be squalid, but they will live and die free. Of course, there may also be a certain degree of pride involved, a rewriting of the 1945 defeat and subsequent American occupation almost a half a century after said events. Suspicion surrounding the intentions of an international fleet is hardly a new theme, seeing as it also shows up in *Japan Sinks*. It is the Capsule's city, and this idea is explored in the last frames of the manga. The destroyed buildings spontaneously straighten as Kaneda passes by at maximum speed, followed by the spirits of Tetsuo and Yamagata. We are reminded of *Crazy Thunder Road* and Jin's comment about riding a motorcycle with no brakes: "Where I'm going, I don't need them."

On a more cynical note, Kaneda's attitude may signal his acceptance of a never-ending cycle of violence. There is no guarantee that the Great Akira Empire will be any more humane, stable, or just than Neo-Tokyo at the

9. Joseph Kitagawa. *Religion in Japanese History*. Columbia University Press, 1990.

height of its glory (and this is true whether or not it is Kaneda who goes on to build it). After all, weren't the brutal economic and social disparities of the megalopolis replaced by an even crueler and more bloodthirsty regime after Akira's second awakening? And perhaps Kaneda doesn't actually intend to build anything at all. A selfish nihilism may be lurking behind his thirst for freedom. Could posturing wind up being more important to him than planning? No one really knows. At any rate, cesspool or not, the Great Akira Empire belongs to the survivors. In Kenzaburo Oe's first novel *Nip the Buds, Shoot the Kids* (1958), fifteen rogue teenagers are left to their own devices in a village deserted by its inhabitants. The plague has already killed off much of the population. Although the adolescents are only left alone for a few days, the hero and his comrades go through a series of formative experiences: first love, first hunt, first burial, etc. When the adults return, they desecrate the graves to incinerate the corpses within, before admonishing the kids for having plundered the few provisions they'd left behind. Witnessing the bodies being dug up truly afflicts the children, who had learned firsthand about death, mourning, and the responsibility of coping with such heartbreak as a group. They are symbolically deprived of an experience that, however cruel and sordid, belonged to them and them alone. "Their" funeral ritual was charged with meaning: it was the symbolism needed to unite the group. Desecration tears this unity apart. This is arguably what Kaneda means when he tells the international forces that "the memory of Akira lives in his heart." Neo-Tokyo may be in ruins, but the significance of this terrifying experience must be preserved and respected. It would be wrong to defile it through foreign intervention.

THE IMPACT OF
AKIRA

A MANGA
[R]EVOLUTION

2.7: Creature: Tetsuo (Final Phase), Transcendence and the Divine Child

O NE WOULD THINK that Tetsuo's newfound authority would satisfy his ego. Both venerated and feared, he essentially rules over the Great Tokyo Empire, but his privileged status makes little difference. Haunted by the same demons, he continues to ignore the warning signals generated by his subconscious mind. Not only did hubris trigger his metamorphosis, it continues to dictate all of his actions. Tetsuo has neither matured nor evolved, and his new rank is unlikely to put an end to his neurotic compulsions. The young man refuses to acknowledge any burdensome thoughts, preferring to avoid introspection and emotionally close himself off. It will take a key figure to unlock Tetsuo's heart and mind (insofar as this is possible). And indeed, only one person is capable of helping Tetsuo face his repressed feelings, and this individual is Kaori.

In the film, Tetsuo's timid girlfriend is reduced to the role of a bit player, one who doesn't seem to have the slightest hold over her boyfriend. And while the anime suggests a certain bond—with Tetsuo belatedly asking for Kaori's assistance—their relationship is a far cry from the one portrayed in the manga. In the latter, the frail young woman meets Tetsuo after he has founded the Great Tokyo Empire. A survivor of the recent disaster that has destroyed the megalopolis, she is painstakingly searching through the rubble in the hope of finding food for herself and her injured father. Tetsuo's aide spots her in the throng of inhabitants seeking rations. He tells her that she could vastly improve her living conditions if she were to "serve" his boss. Being both docile and innocent, Kaori is coerced into joining the regime, although she has no idea what this entails. Unbeknownst to her, she is to be Tetsuo's sex slave and soon finds herself in a state of undress. She and two other "lucky" girls are presented to "Master Tetsuo," who offers each of them a drug-laden capsule before they "give themselves" to him.

This acid-fueled orgy, which is all about power and domination, is most likely Tetsuo's first sexual encounter. And like the warlord of a conquered territory, he accepts the virgins gifted to him. This isn't just about the pleasures of the flesh: it's Tetsuo's ego that's truly being stroked. Having taken the drug, the other two girls die, but Kaori—who only pretended to swallow her dose—is spared. Tetsuo, who loathes insubordination, is curiously tolerant when it comes to Kaori. As for the young woman, she isn't at all fooled by Tetsuo's virile displays of power. And although she is never openly defiant, she doesn't seem to be the least bit afraid of Tetsuo. Kaori sees him for who he really is: a vulnerable and lonely young man. And, much to the chagrin of his aide (who fears that Kaori's influence outweighs his own), Tetsuo is no longer interested in having his own personal "harem." Tetsuo truly relies on Kaori, whom he sees as a girlfriend, confidante, and maternal substitute.

Nevertheless, the solace that she provides has its limits. Believing in his own invincibility, Tetsuo makes the mistake of probing Akira's mind. This gives him a terrible shock, and the terror he experiences is unlike anything he has ever known. He obviously covets Akira's powers. Knowing that they are of a completely different magnitude than his own makes him both unhappy and impatient. Traumatized by said "encounter," Tetsuo makes his first sound decision since the awakening of his psychic powers. He decides to seek out and question Lady Miyako. He still hates to admit to weakness, and is thus noticeably ill at ease. Miyako tells him what she knows about the Akira project. This is how Tetsuo learns that his thinking is faulty: he sees things in two dimensions as opposed to Akira, who is able to perceive a four (or even five) dimensional plane. The teenager's limited perception leads him to believe that his powers are subject to a linear progression. It's as if they had to respond to some quantifiable logic. After explaining that Akira's mind isn't a part of the universe's natural movement, Lady Miyako elaborates that: "People who are trapped in the universal flow will never understand." The symbolism behind Miyako's blindness is evident. It highlights the need to reject the physical world's sterility and look at reality differently. Only then can one become consciously aware of the infinite number of possibilities. Because Lady Miyako is blind, she is not duped by sensory illusions. She sees existence and the nature of the flow quite clearly.

Meanwhile, Tetsuo is indeed caught up in that which is material. He takes drugs, not only to develop and control his nascent power, but also to keep his demons at bay. Miyako is emphatic when she says that this simplistic solution limits Tetsuo's psychic power. She tells him that the drugs "expedite the release of [his] mental energies, but that they are just a short cut," adding that "when [he] can overcome [his] own weakness, the power will flow from [him] freely." Tetsuo thus faces a fundamental dilemma, one that he'd rather ignore: his addiction is intimately linked to his neurotic compulsions. Weaning himself off the drug would open the tried and tested floodgates of his unconscious mind, thus eliminating the very substance that helps him bury his fears. And while Tetsuo's anger masks his denial, he still knows that Miyako is right.

His first attempt at withdrawal is short-lived. Being a true addict, the prospect of intense short-term suffering is more terrifying than surrender, even though the drug offers shorter and shorter periods of respite. Relentlessly attacked by both his body and mind, Tetsuo's sleep is chock-full of inner demons. His dreams revolve around his childhood, his relationship with Kaneda, and his addiction, and this is true even before his attempts to wean himself off the powerful substance. In the end, it's too much of an effort, and the teenager stuffs himself with capsules once again. His act is the natural consequence of self-disgust. While Kaori readily accepts Tetsuo's foibles, he cannot tolerate his own imperfections. He mistakenly believes that the burden he carries—the venomous poison weighing on his mind—is his own weakness. This couldn't be further from the truth: his affliction is pride and the ensuing denial of his flaws. If he cannot accept his inadequacies, his neuroses will continue to torture him.

Tetsuo finally makes a radical move and chucks out his entire supply of capsules. He's all in now: he'll let the chips fall where they may. And while he initially seems serene, this is only because the burden of choice no longer weighs upon him. He cannot escape the distressful symptoms of withdrawal. Once these symptoms get the better of him, he sets off to ask Miyako for more capsules. She refuses and tells him that he must come to terms with his own suffering, that this is his "destiny." When the Satellite Orbital Laser fires and illuminates the skyline, Tetsuo has a vision. The satellite's blast creates a rift in the clouds, forming a gateway that allows him to see the "flow." This serves as a trigger, opening his mind, and the teenager experiences his first genuine metaphysical experience. The veil of the physical world is torn asunder for a brief moment, enabling Tetsuo to contemplate the flow. He witnesses his own birth and catches a glimpse of the same double helix conjured up by Akira: it represents DNA, the driving force of evolution. Tetsuo then sees the little boy smiling at him in the illuminated sky. The teenager has taken his first step toward understanding the universal flow, a crucial move if he is to control his power.

Unfortunately, this moment of transcendence brings Kaneda back from whatever dimension he had been sent to following Akira's second awakening. This rekindles Tetsuo's jealousy and ultimately compromises the odds of any further progression.

No one knows where Akira and Tetsuo went during their brief absence. No one knows what secrets the little boy revealed to the teenager, who seems to be transformed upon his return. Tetsuo is cleaner, his hair is shorter, and he seems at peace with himself, so much so that his aide barely recognizes him. But as soon as he returns to his quarters, Tetsuo hides behind Kaori's skirts, visibly weakened by his recent experience. He has touched that which is untouchable and has not returned unscathed.

Tetsuo finally understands the meaning of Miyako's words and the nature of the "flow." And while his personal issues remain unresolved, the teenager realizes that a power like Akira's cannot be controlled by flexing one's muscles and gritting one's teeth. Letting go, surrendering himself to the flow of universal energy, is his first step toward transcendence. In sum, Miyako was right: his own limitations prevented him from truly comprehending Akira, no matter how hard he scrutinized him. When he goes to pay a "courtesy" visit to the international scientists hanging out near the Japanese coast, Tetsuo speaks of the material world and its opposition to that which lies beyond. He tells them that "the truth and *[their]* science are in completely different dimensions."

And then comes the great gathering, the jam-packed rally that resembles a holy mass in honor of Akira. It is supposed to restore the morale of the troops and send a clear message to the Great Empire's enemies. For Tetsuo, this event is clearly the point of no return. Wanting to show off his newfound abilities, he bites off a bit more than he can chew. He flies off and lands on the moon. And unlike Neil Armstrong, he's not taking a "giant leap for mankind." He is there to tear a hole in the celestial body, an act that has both an immediate and dramatic impact on the Earth. While lunar debris rains down on the city, the disruption to the tides causes a massive tsunami, killing many of those who support the Great Tokyo Empire.

For whom was this demonstration intended? Was Akira attempting to find out if Tetsuo could control his powers? It's hard to say. But even Miyako believes that Tetsuo has gone too far. His body is beginning to show disturbing signs of a mutation that will only worsen over time. The initial symptoms appear in the exact spot where he was first injured, i.e. his arm, which has been prosthetic ever since it was severed. New muscles, tendons, and nerves develop and fuse with the scrap metal, pipes, and cables of his robotic arm. This complete loss of regenerative control is the result of his ferocious appetite for power. Tetsuo's body is basically eating him alive.

In the manga, the teenager's mutation goes through several phases before he morphs into the huge mass of pink flesh that we see in the film. But in both versions, he ultimately winds up looking like a gigantic infant-like blob. Even Miyako isn't sure what this means: is there a rebirth involved? Or is Tetsuo returning to humankind's very first developmental stage? Not only does the symbolism surrounding infants tend to validate both interpretations, it also gives rise to many others. And while it would be foolhardy to ignore these multiple levels of analysis, we essentially see the infant as a symbol of both the unconscious and infinite possibility. In the latter case, newborns embody potential, because the idea of growth is inevitably associated with them. Babies do not remain the same, and their development is associated with a vital form of energy. Mythological heroes and prophets are often the result of miraculous births, events celebrated as signs of providence: the story of Jesus Christ is undoubtedly the best example of this.

And the concept of the unconscious is even more thought-provoking, because it allows us to better understand Akira himself. In the manga, children are much more adept at developing their "power." The Swiss psychiatrist Carl Jung (1875-1961) laid the basis for this comparison when he wrote that, "The phenomenology of the 'child's' birth always points back to an original psychological state of non-recognition, i.e., of darkness or twilight, of non-differentiation between subject and object, of [the] unconscious identity of man and the universe."[1] Jung is referring to the fact that very young children have not yet developed a sense of self, meaning that their relationship to the world remains perfectly abstract. And if we continue to follow Jung's train of thought, the infant's lack of self-identity can be traced back to the notion that the child is still "one" with the mother. This means that the infant still has one foot firmly planted in the unconscious, "the only available source of religious experience" according to Jung. He goes on to explain that what we call the unconscious is not synonymous with God. It is "simply the medium from which religious experience seems to flow. [...]. Knowledge of God is a transcendental problem."[2] The young Akira no longer has an ego nor a conscience. Miyako believes that he is an empty shell. But this is precisely what allows the little boy to channel his "power." Consciousness—the realm of language, reason, and thought—can only interpret (and thus distort) that which is inexplicable, that eternal absolute that Tetsuo briefly catches a glimpse of. He differentiates between science and the truth, basically telling the scientists that their activity is equivalent to relying on consciousness to explain its opposite. Absolute truth eludes language, since the latter is a material and conscious form of expression. Buddha does not attempt to explain the nature of Nirvana, because it would be impossible. He can only offer advice on how to achieve it. Among Hindus, Brahman (the ultimate reality) is indefinable: any attempt to do so would be a misrepresentation. In *Akira*, both the "flow" and "power" seem to be of a similar nature. They are absolute, transcendent truths, too profound to be consciously understood. The image of the infant is thus a symbol of the unconscious, a form of transcendence that is

1. Carl Gustav Jung. *Collected Works.* Vol. 9, Princeton University Press, 1969.
2. Carl Gustav Jung. *Collected Works.* Vol. 10, Princeton University Press, 1981.

similar to the one we see at the end of Stanley Kubrick's *2001, A Space Odyssey*. In this film, the protagonist comes into contact with a mysterious black monolith and subsequently finds himself transformed into a cosmic baby/fetus.

THE IMPACT OF

AKIRA

A MANGA
[R]EVOLUTION

2.8: Creature: Conclusion,
Akira and the Collapse

S O, WHAT ARE WE TO MAKE OF *AKIRA*? In this book, we have attempted to unravel the mysteries of its author, the genesis of his work, and the story itself. Nevertheless, we are still unable to come up with a simple response (or indeed any response at all) to the elementary question: what's it all about?

Beyond our desire to pay tribute to the masterpiece and its creator, the yearning to answer this question was what gave rise to this publication in the first place. But even after months of obsessive work, analyzing both the manga and the film, there doesn't appear to be any solution that will help us untangle its underlying meaning.

We finally remembered Saya Shiraishi's quote, the one about original experiences and how they refuse rhetorical elucidation. Tying to sum up *Akira* in a few sentences is pointless. A synopsis of the film's first few minutes or the manga's introductory pages would say nothing about the work as a whole. It would be like reading a review of Beethoven's *9th*, a Wikipedia summary of *Hamlet*, or the back of a Blu-ray description of *Pulp Fiction*. We might even go so far as to say that it would be misleading. And perhaps this is what makes Akira so viral, what anchors it in pop culture, even today. You don't explain it to the uninitiated, you show it to them. You share it. Only afterward is deliberation possible.

The second part of this book, dedicated to the analysis of *Akira*, opens with the memories of Hiroshima and Nagasaki, as well as a discussion of the atomic bomb's predominance in post-war fiction, but this is merely because Neo-Tokyo has been subjected to a series of explosions. Nevertheless, these explosions are not *Akira*'s main subject, the principal theme that would allow us to understand the work in its entirety. All of *Akira*'s themes are interconnected. They echo, reinforce, and even fuel one another. The manga's very structure responds to this logic, since several stories intertwine without any one character becoming the star.

Akira's complexity prevents it from being fully grasped: it would be like pretending to have a global view of our environment, to see it from a 360° perspective. We seize upon the fragments of the whole and analyze them, but their endless and subtle connections lie out of reach. This is also what leads to multiple viewings and readings. We never have one "definitive" reaction. We emerge from the tale shaken, seduced, terrified, and even shocked: we experience a cocktail of emotions, the polar opposite of indifference. And this impermanence of feeling, this perpetual struggle between contradictory feelings, is what we call fascination.

If we take a step back and consider the bigger picture, it is perhaps possible to see a link, an underlying dynamic that connects all of *Akira*'s themes and protagonists: the idea of collapse. Like many cyberpunk works, there is an end-of-the-century malaise haunting the streets of Neo-Tokyo. It points to the implosion of a system whose logic is dying, because it is no longer able to bear the weight of its own contradictions.

The detonator is Tetsuo. The teenager is the symbol (and symptom) of failure from both above and below. He is pulled in two different directions—by two irreconcilable worlds—and thus represents the breaking point, the domino that sets everything in motion. Let's first look at the failure from below. Neo-Tokyo's society is both fragile and deeply sick. Its destabilization is apparent in even its smallest cell, that of the family. Tetsuo is an uprooted and abandoned teen, left to fend for himself at an age when children need a solid base, a home. There isn't a traditional united family to be found, and this is true in both the film and the manga. We see gangs of delinquents trying to kill one another and overindulging in self-destructive ways. We see large demonstrations against ill-suited economic reforms, proposed by an elite that is totally out of touch with the people and their needs. We witness the rise of apocalyptic cults, which the most nihilistic members of society join because they are searching for a semblance of meaning in their existence. Neo-Tokyo is a trompe-l'oeil: it is no longer a flashy megalopolis, it is a chaotic jungle where the "group" no longer exists, where social conventions have become vestigial remnants, and where orphans emerge in the twilight of a world whose pretenses are slowly destroying it.

And then there is the failure from above. It takes the form of the politicians' crass incompetence and the scientists' madness. The latter should have learned from their past mistakes, but their ego is such that they keep repeating them instead. The army scientists almost blew up the entire planet by playing God and abandoning ethics. Thirty years later, the memory of the catastrophe does little to discourage them from tempting the devil a second time.

Those at the top are dismissive of the pleading cries from below, so much so that those cries soon become warlike in nature. By continuing to pursue Eden (or perhaps Babylon)—by forging ahead in their attempts to create a new "augmented and perfected" human master species—the scientists make their megalomania known. Is it fate, a self-fulfilling prophecy, that led to Tetsuo? They gave him everything he needed to implode, resulting in an inevitable downward spiral.

Akira is a tale about societal collapse. It is about a spectacular and tragic ending, and its message still resonates, perhaps now more than ever. Katsuhiro Otomo's work reflects historical truths. It evokes terrible memories and warns us of history's (perpetual) repetitions. Thirty years after the film adaptation, the lights of Neo-Tokyo continue to fascinate us. And we admire them, in spite of our fears. We gleefully allow ourselves to be entertained by the nightmarish tale. Why? Because *"Akira* is violent, and it is beautiful."

THE IMPACT OF
AKIRA

A MANGA
[R]EVOLUTION

Bibliography

Books:

Benedict, Ruth. *Le Chrysanthème et le Sabre*. Éditions Philippe Picquier, Collection Picquier Poche, 1998.

Bouissou, Jean-Marie. *Manga - Histoire et Univers de la Bande Dessinée Japonaise*. Éditions Philippe Picquier, Collection Picquier Poche, 2013.

Dowsey, Stuart J. *Zengakuren: Japan's Revolutionary Students*. Ishi Press, 2012.

Dubois, Romain, Ludovic Gottigny, and Malik-Djamel Amazigh Houha. *Rockyrama Hors-Série Akira*. Ynnis Éditions, Collection YNI.LIVRES, 2019.

Evans, Richard I., Carl Gustav Jung, and Ernest Jones, *Conversations with Carl Jung & Reactions from Ernest Jones*. D. Van Nostrand Company, 1964.

Haghirian, Parissa. *Understanding Japanese Management Practices*. Business Expert Press, 2010.

Jung, Carl Gustav. *Collected Works*. Vol. 9, Princeton University Press, 1969.

Jung, Carl Gustav. *Collected Works*. Vol. 10, Princeton University Press, 1981.

Katzenstein, Peter J. and Takashi Shiraishi. *Network Power: Japan and Asia*. Cornell University Press, 1997. Quote from Chapter 7, "Japan's Soft Power: Doraemon Goes Overseas," by Saya Shiraishi.

Kitagawa, Joseph M. *Religion in Japanese History*. Columbia University Press, 1990.

Laplantine, François. *Le Japon ou le Sens des Extrêmes*. Éditions Pocket, Collection Agora, 2017.

Mitsui, Toru. *Made in Japan: Studies in Popular Music*. Routledge, Routledge Global Popular Music Series, 2015.

Murakami, Takashi. *Little Boy: The Arts of Japan's Exploding Subculture*. Yale University Press, 2005.

Nakamura, Hajime. *Ways of Thinking of Eastern Peoples: India, China, Tibet, Japan*. University of Hawaii Press, 1980.

Nakane, Chie. *Japanese Society*. Pelican, 1970.

Otomo, Katsuhiro. *Akira Club*. Kodansha, 1995.

Otomo, Katsuhiro. *KABA - 1971-1989 ILLUSTRATION COLLECTION*. Kodansha, 1989.

Poupée, Karyn. *Histoire du Manga*. Éditions Tallandier, Collection Texto, 2016.

Poupée, Karyn. *Les Japonais*. Éditions Tallandier, Collection Texto, 2012.

Redmond, Sean. *Liquid Metal: The Science Fiction Film Reader*. Columbia University Press, 2004.

Sato, Ikuya. *Kamikaze Biker: Parody and Anomy in Affluent Japan*. University of Chicago Press, 1991.

Williams, Peter and David Wallace. *La Guerre Bactériologique: Les Secrets des Expérimentations Japonaises*. Éditions Albin Michel, 1990.

Articles:

Andrews, William. "Political Comics: Japan Radicalism and New Left Protest Movement Told Through Manga." *Throw Out Your Books*, 3 Nov. 2015, throwoutyourbooks.wordpress.com/2015/11/03/political-comics-japan-radicalism-pro-test-movements-manga/.

Ashcraft, Brian. "Why Big, Badass Robots (and Mecha) Rule Japan." *Kotaku.com*, 25 Aug. 2011, kotaku.com/why-big-badass-robots-and-mecha-rule-japan-5834287.

Beier, Lars-Olav and Tobias Rapp. Nora Reinhardt. "Fairytales of the Apocalypse - Hayao Miyazaki's Prophetic Whimsy." *Der Spiegle*, 24 Mar. 2011, www.spiegel.de/international/zeitgeist/fairy-tales-of-the-apocalypse-hayao-miyazaki-s-pro-phetic-whimsy-a-752710.html.

Berthon, Jean-Pierre and Naoki Kashio. "Les Nouvelles Voies Spirituelles au Japon : État des Lieux et Mutations de la Religiosité." *Archive des Sciences Sociales des Religions*, 109, janvier-mars [Jan.-Mar.] 2000, journals.openedition.org/assr/20176.

Bouissou, Jean-Marie. "Manga Goes Global." *Critique Internationale*, 7 (Culture Populaire et Politique), 2000, www.persee.fr/doc/criti_1290-7839_2000_num_7_1_1577.

"Portrait Katsuhiro Otomo le révolutionnaire." *Bounthavy.com*, 30 Jan. 2015, bounthavy.com/wordpress/portrait-katsuhiro-otomo-le-revolutionnaire/.

Broderick, Michael. "Superflat Eschatology." *Animation Studies*, 12 July 2009, journal.animationstudies.org/michael-broderick-superflat-eschatology/.

Brothers, David. "Katsuhiro Otomo and the Perfect Panels of *Akira*." *Comics Alliance.com*, 24 June 2011, comicsalliance.com/katsuhiro-otomo-akira/.

Callahan, Kat. "The *Bosozoku* are Japan's Disappearing Rebels Without a Cause." *Jalopnik.com*, 4 Oct. 2014, jalopnik.com/the-bosozoku-are-japans-disappearing-rebels-without-a-c-1642416129.

Carson-Byrne, Maxine. "Kusunoki Masashige: Loyal to the End." *Stories from the Museum Floor*, 13 July 2018, storiesfromthemuseumfloor.wordpress.com/2018/07/13/kusunoki-masashige-loyal-to-the-end/.

Cartledge, S.T. "Rebuilding Neo-Tokyo: The Search of Normality in the Apocalypse of Akira." 20 Jan. 2012, themanifold.wordpress.com/2012/01/20/rebuilding-neo-tokyo-the-search-for-normality-in-the-apocalypse-of-akira/.

"Comment les manga sont-ils arrivés en France ?" *Le Chapelier Fou*, 7 Aug. 2013, fouchapelier.wordpress.com/2013/08/07/comment-les-manga-sont-ils-arrives-en-france/.

Chira, Susan. "Tokyo Journal; Motto for a new Breed; Less Work and More Play." *The New York Times*, 25 Jan. 1988, www.nytimes.com/1988/01/25/world/tokyo-journal-motto-for-a-new-breed-less-work-and-more-play.html.

Clements, Jonathan. "Manga and the Bomb." *Aljazeera America*, 8 Aug. 2015, america.aljazeera.com/articles/2015/8/8/manga-and-the-bomb.html.

Cyhowski, Jared. "Editorial: On Akira and its Existence in Japanese Cinema." *Operationrainfall. com*, 18 Nov. 2013, operationrainfall.com/2013/11/18/akira-existence-japanese-cinema/#japanamerica.

Cherrybomb. "The Wild Wild World of Japanese Rebel Biker Culture." *Dangerous Minds*, 28 May 2015, dangerousminds.net/comments/japanese_rebel_biker_culture.

Davis, Antonix. "Subcultures and Sociology: Bosozoku." *Grinnell College*, haenfler.sites.grinnell.edu/subcultures-and-scenes/bosozoku/.

Downer, Lesley. "Waiting for Disaster is a Way of Life in Japan." *The Telegraph*, 11 Mar. 2011, www.telegraph.co.uk/comment/8377303/Waiting-for-disaster-is-a-way-of-life-in-Japan.html.

Drucker, Peter F. "Behind Japan's Success." *Harvard Business Review*, Jan. 1981, hbr.org/1981/01/behind-japans-success.

"Steamboy, Notes de Production." Elbakin.net/fantasy/cinema/production_steamboy.htm.

Frost, Peter. "Postwar Japan, 1952-1989." *Japan Society*, 2003, aboutjapan.japansociety.org/content.cfm/postwar_japan_1952-1989#sthash.ml0nGrEk.nSfhxdv5.dpbs.

Fueller, Frank. "The Atomic Bomb: Reflections in Japanese Manga and Anime." May 2012, radar.auctr.edu/islandora/object/cau.td%3A2012_fuller_frank_r?search=-atomic%2520bomb.

Fueller, Frank. "The Deep Influence of the A-Bomb on Anime and Manga." *The Conversation*, 6 Aug. 2015, theconversation.com/the-deep-influence-of-the-a-bomb-on-anime-and-manga-45275.

Gates, James. "The Origin of Japan's Obsession with Giant Robots." *Theculturetrip.com*, 3 Aug. 2018, theculturetrip.com/asia/japan/articles/mech-ing-a-big-deal-of-it-japans-obsession-with-giant-robots/.

Gibson, William. "The Future Perfect." *Time*, 30 Apr. 2001, content.time.com/time/magazine/article/0,9171,1956774,00.html.

Gravett, Paul. "Katsuhiro Otomo, Post-Apocalypse Now." *Comic Heroes Magazine*, no. 19, Future Publishing, 2013.

Hale, Michael. "The Comics Classroom: AKIRA, a Cyberpunk Masterpiece." *Comicosity.com*, 20 June 2019, www.comicosity.com/the-comics-classroom-akira-a-cyberpunk-masterpiece/.

Kober, Marc. "Récits du Corps au Japon." *Itinéraires*, 2011-3, 2011, journals.openedition.org/itineraires/1487#ftn19.

Lahiri, Hiranmoy. "Reality through Fantasy: Miyazaki Hayao's 'Anime' Films." *The Asian-Pacific Journal: Japan Focus*, vol. 12, issue 39, no. 2, 28 Sept. 2014, apjjf.org/2014/12/39/Hiranmoy-Lahiri/4191/article.html.

Leong, Anthony. "Those Who are About to Die: Battle Royale." *Asian Cult Cinema*, no. 33, Nov. 2001.

Oguma, Eiji. "An Industry Awaiting Reform: The Social Origins and Economics of Manga and Animation in Postwar Japan." *The Asia-Pacific Journal: Japan Focus*, translated by Yokota Kayoko, vol. 15, issue 9, no. 1, 27 Apr. 2017, apjjf.org/2017/09/Oguma.html.

Oguma, Eiji. "Japan's 1968: A Collective Reaction to Rapid Economic Growth in Age of Turmoil." *The Asia-Pacific Journal: Japan Focus*, translated by Nick Kapur with Samuel Malissa and Stephen Polandvol, vol. 13, issue 12, no. 1, 23 Mar. 2015, apjjf.org/2015/13/11/Oguma-Eiji/4300.html.

Oguma, Eiji. "What Was 'The 1968 Movement?' Japan's Experience in a Global Perspective." *The Asia-Pacific Journal: Japan Focus*, vol. 16, issue 11, no. 6, 1 June 2018, apjjf.org/2018/11/Oguma.html.

Osaki, Tomohiro. "Worn to be Wild: Tokkofuku Combat Uniforms." *Japantimes.co.jp*, 8 Sept. 2018, www.japantimes.co.jp/life/2018/09/08/style/worn-wild-tokkofuku-combat-%E2%80%A8u-niforms/#.XUf7pegzbEi.

Osmond, Andrew. "Akira: The Story Behind the Film." *Empire*, 21 June 2011, www.empireonline.com/movies/features/story-behind-film-akira/.

Penney, Matthew. "War and Japan: The Non-Fiction Manga of Mizuki Shigeru." *The Asia-Pacific Journal: Japan Focus*, vol. 6, issue 9, 1 Sept. 2008, apjjf.org/-Matthew-Penney/2905/article.html.

Sato, Ikuya. "Crime and Play as Excitement: A Conceptual Analysis of Japanese Bosozoku (Motorcycle Gangs)." *Tohoku Psychologica Folia*, vol. 41, 22 Mar. 1983.

Sato, Kumiko. "From Hello Kitty to Cod Roe Kewpie - A Postwar Cultural History of Cuteness in Japan." *Asian Intercultural Contacts*, vol. 14, no. 2, Autumn 2009, www.asianstudies.org/publications/eaa/archives/from-hello-kitty-to-cod-roe-kewpie-a-post-war-cultural-history-of-cuteness-in-japan/.

Schley, Matt. "'Akira' Looking Back at the Future." *The Japan Times*, October 2018, features.japantimes.co.jp/akira-new/.

Schley, Matt. "Speak Japanese like an 'Akira' Biker Punk." *The Japan Times*, October 2018, features.japantimes.co.jp/akiraweek-bilingual/.

Schreiber, Mark. "Lucky Dragon's Lethal Catch." *The Japan Times*, 18 Mar. 2012, www.japantimes.co.jp/life/2012/03/18/general/lucky-dragons-lethal-catch/#.XUayAegzbEg.

Schupp, Ricky. "Japan's Violent Motorcycle Gangs That Influenced Akira - and Anime History." *Tokyo Weekender*, 11 Dec. 2018, www.tokyoweekender.com/2018/12/japans-violent-motorcycle-gangs-influenced-akira/.

Spicer, Paul. "Bosozoku: Society, Politics, and Terror." *Think.iafor.org*, 9 Feb. 2016, think.iafor.org/bosozuku-society-politics-and-terror/.

"Akira (Film Essay)." 26 May 2011, slamdunkstudios.webs.com/apps/blog/show/22844873-akira-film-essay-.

Takekuma, Kentaro. "Japanese Lecture/Blog Post Translation: The Space Between Anime and Manga: #5: Katsuhiro Otomo, the Anti-'Story.'" Translated by Kransom, *2chan.us*, 17 May 2009, 2chan.us/wordpress/2009/05/17/japanese-lectureblog-post-translation-the-space-between-anime-and-manga-5-katsuhiro-otomo-the-anti-story-author-by-kentaro-takekuma/.

Tanaka, Yuki. "War and Peace in the Art of Tezuka Osamu: The Humanism of his Epic Manga." *The Asia-Pacific Journal: Japan Focus*, vol. 8, issue 38, no. 1, 20 Sept. 2010, apjjf.org/-Yuki-Tanaka/3412/article.html.

Tatsumi, Takayuki. "Transpacific Cyperpunk: Transgeneric Interactions Between Prose, Cinema, and Manga." *Arts*, 2 Mar. 2018, researchgate.net/publication/323530707_Transpacific_Cyberpunk_Transgeneric_Interactions_between_Prose_Cinema_and_Manga.

Tran, John L. "1968: The Year Japan Truly Raised its Voice." *The Japan Times*, 19 Nov. 2017, www.japantimes.co.jp/culture/2017/11/19/arts/1968-year-japan-truly-raised-voice/#.XUf-aOgzbEh.

Trinh, Sylvaine. "Aum Shinrikyô: Secte et Violence (Parties 1 - 3)." *Cultures & Conflits* 29-30, Automne-Hiver [Autumn-Winter] 1998, journals.openedition.org/conflits/718. journals.openedition.org/conflits/720. journals.openedition.org/conflits/722.

Usher, Tom. "How 'Akira' Has Influenced All Your Favourite TV, Film and Music." *Vice*, 21 Sept. 2016, www.vice.com/en_uk/article/kwk55w/how-akira-has-influenced-modern-culture.

Wolken, Lawrence C. "The Modernization of an Ancient Culture: Post War Japan." *Mays Business School, Texas A&M University*, maysweb.tamu.edu/sage/gradescourses/9th-12th-grade/economics/the-modernization-of-an-ancient-culture-preface/.

"Bosozoku: The Craziest Autos in the World." 25 Aug. 2017, yabai.com/p/3110.

Interviews:

Aoki, Deb. "Akira in Color with Steve Oliff." *Animenewsnetwork.com*, 17 Mar. 2016, www.animenewsnetwork.com/interview/2016-03-17/akira-in-color-with-steve-oliff/.99830.

Aoki, Deb. "Bridging the Gap Between US Comics and Manga with Kodansha USA." *Animenewsnetwork.com*, 5 Nov. 2015, www.animenewsnetwork.com/feature/2015-11-05/bridging-the-gap-between-us-comics-and-manga-with-kodansha-usa/.95039.

"Special Interview - Katsuhiro Otomo." 15 Aug. 2013,
asianbeat.com/en/feature/issue_anime/otomo/interview.html.

Barder, Ollie. *"Katsuhiro Otomo on Creating 'Akira' and Designing the Coolest Bike in all of Manga and Anime."* Forbes, *26 May 2017*,
www.forbes.com/sites/olliebarder/2017/05/26/katsuhiro-otomo-on-creating-akira-and-designing-the-coolest-bike-in-all-of-manga-and-anime/#3d7f83506d25.

Baud, Hélène. "'Steamboy': Rencontre avec Katsuhiro Otomo." *Allociné.fr*, 17 Sept. 2004,
www.allocine.fr/article/fichearticle_gen_carticle=18366151.html.

Beaujean, Stéphane. "ENERGY, CONCENTRATION, HONESTY: The Making of *Akira* in the Words of Katsuhiro Otomo." Transcript from 9 Jan. 2019 interview in the magazine *KABOOM*, no. 13, Feb.-Apr. 2016,
kodanshacomics.com/2019/01/09/10-years-kodansha-comics-akira/.

Brutus Magazine. "A Conversation Between Katsuhiro Otomo and Takehiko Inoue." Translated by Mangabrog, *Mangabrog.wordpress.com*, 13 Nov. 2004,
mangabrog.wordpress.com/2014/11/13/a-conversation-between-katsuhiro-otomo-and-take-hiko-inoue/.

CasaBrutus. "Naoki Urasawa Interview Part 1 & 2." Translated by DrSenbei, *Tokyoscums. blogspot.com*, 27 Aug. 2009,
tokyoscum.blogspot.com/2009/08/naoki-urasawa-interview-part-1.html.
tokyoscum.blogspot.com/2009/08/naoki-urasawa-interview-part-2.html.

Chapuis, Marius. "KATSHUIRO OTOMO: 'JE NE ME PRÉOCCUPE PAS DES AUTRES.'" *Libération*, 27 Jan. 2016,
next.liberation.fr/livres/2016/01/27/katsuhiro-otomo-je-ne-me-preoccupe-pas-des-autres_1429354.

Jarno, Stéphane. "Katsuhiro Otomo: 'Akira est une œuvre antisystème.'" *Telerama*, 17 June 2016.
www.telerama.fr/livre/katsuhiro-otomo-akira-est-une-oeuvre-antisysteme,144046.php.

"Naoki Urasawa and Hisashi Eguchi Talk about Manga in the 70s and 80s, Mostly Otomo." Translated by Mangabrog, *Mangabrog.wordpress.com*, 17 May 2015,
mangabrog.wordpress.com/2015/05/17/naoki-urasawa-and-hisashi-eguchi-talk-about-man-ga-in-the-70s-and-80s-mostly-otomo/.

Médioni, Gilles. "Otomo: les maîtres de la BD qui l'ont influencé," *L'Express.fr*, 25 July 2005,
www.lexpress.fr/culture/livre/otomo-et-ses-bandes_820650.html.

Nakazawa, Keiji. "Barefoot Gen, The Atomic Bomb and I: The Hiroshima Legacy." Interview with Asai Motofumi, translated by Richard H. Minear, *The Asia-Pacific Journal: Japan Focus*, vol. 6, issue 1, 1 Jan. 2006,
apjjf.org/-Nakazawa-Keiji/2638/article.html.

Navas, David. "A Conversation between Katsuhiro Otomo and Koji Morimoto." *Davidnavas. com*, 11 Sept. 2017,
www.davidnavas.com/blog/2012/11/11/a-conversation-between-katsuhiro-otomo-anb-koji-morimoto.

Orsini, Alexis. "Katsuhiro Ôtomo vu par Naoki Urasawa." *Labasesecrete.fr*, 26 Jan. 2016,
labasesecrete.fr/katsuhiro-otomo-vu-par-naoki-urasawa/.

"Katsuhiro Otomo." Interview with *The Onion*, by Tasha Robinson, *Film.avclub.com*, 6 Apr. 2005,
film.avclub.com/katsuhiro-otomo-1798208474.

"Interview: Alejandro Jodorowsky (L'Étrange Festival)." Interview with *FilmActu*, by Yann Rutledge, *Cinema.jeuxactu.com*, 5 Nov. 2010, cinema.jeuxactu.com/interview-cinema-interview-alejandro-jodorowsky-l-etrange-festival-11631.htm.

Sato, Kuriko. "Katsuhiro Otomo." *Midnighteye.com*, 29 Dec. 2006, www.midnighteye.com/interviews/katsuhiro-otomo/.

Sevakis, Justin. "Katsuhiro Otomo Interview." *Animenewsnetwork.com*, 5 Nov. 2012, www.animenewsnetwork.com/convention/2012/katsuhiro-otomo-interview.

Websites:

"Exploring Akira - *Akira* Resources and Exploration." *WordPress*, exploringakira.wordpress.com/.

Ligonnet, Gérald. "Otomo Katsuhiro, Artiste Japonais." *Ampprod.fr*, otomo.ampprod.fr/otomo-katsuhiro.html.

"Otomo Katsuhiro Chronology." *Chronotomo*, chronotomo.aaandnn.com.

"Site Dedicated to the Art and Comics of Katsuhiro Otomo." *Otomblr*, otomblr.tumblr.com/.

Videos:

Angoulême International Comics Festival. *"À la Rencontre de Katsuhiro Otomo, la Vidéo de l'Événement (FIBD2016) YouTube*, 10 Feb. 2016, www.youtube.com/watch?v=ndXdyon5RW8.

Akira 2019. *Interview with Akira Creator Katsuhiro Otomo (1/4 to 4/4). YouTube*, 29 & 30 Dec. 2009, www.youtube.com/watch?v=nIZZoHF8VmQ. www.youtube.com/watch?v=LOVPrUKh_F4. www.youtube.com/watch?v=_BFmrVHB44w. www.youtube.com/watch?v=uYOzaWJz1vg&t.

Akira 2019. *"Akira (アキラ) Production Report (1988) (English Dub)." YouTube*, 31 Oct. 2018, www.youtube.com/watch?v=gHNtGTu_sEc.

Akira 2019. *"Akira (アキラ) Sounds Clip by Geinoh Yamashirogumi (1/2)." YouTube*, 30 Dec. 2009, www.youtube.com/watch?v=zdSjCBUg8yY.

Anime Eroli. *"Katsuhiro Otomo - Masterpiece of a Mind." YouTube*, 18 Feb. 2017, www.youtube.com/watch?v=MPD8DL-O1E8.

AnimeEveryday. *"The Influence of Akira." YouTube*, 19 May 2016, www.youtube.com/watch?v=8XeBW08HbMk.

Beyond Ghibli. *"Akira & the Masochism of Katsuhiro Otome." YouTube*, 8 Aug. 2018, www.youtube.com/watch?v=Ej9q8Oc4dd0.

Documentary World. *"History Channel - Japan Under American Occupation." YouTube*, 1 Apr. 2017, www.youtube.com/watch?v=grqtxI_MJC0.

Dr. Udru. *"The Bizarreness of Japanese Body Horror."* YouTube, 26 Aug. 2016, www.youtube.com/watch?v=6477Ltn_nI0.

Espace Manga. *"[Conférence] Katsuhiro OTOMO: 'Si je devais refaire Akira aujourd'hui, je ne le referais pas.'"* YouTube, 26 Jan. 2016, www.youtube.com/watch?v=WFyg6MOgmDs.

Felix Comic Art. *STEVE OLIFF: Coloring AKIRA with KATSUHIRO OTOMO.* YouTube, 9 Feb. 2016, www.youtube.com/watch?v=DO-Wo3jFJes.

Haddock39. *"Nippon BBC Documentary 1980s Being Japanese."* YouTube, 27 Aug. 2017, www.youtube.com/watch?v=O_PRwFSozs0.

Ivkovic, Karlo. *"In Search of Moebius (BBC 4 Documentary)."* YouTube, 16 Mar. 2013, www.youtube.com/watch?v=jNas99oEXBU.

Krispies. *Akira: "A Mastery of Violence."* YouTube, 30 Apr. 2017, www.youtube.com/watch?v=3-PYa3dFWkA.

Mowk Tony. *"80s-90s Bosozoku Footage (90 min) HD."* YouTube, 26 June 2016, www.youtube.com/watch?v=K7mUOty-FdQ

Peeters, Benoît. *"Pour une Histoire de la Bande Dessinée: 7/10 Les Métamorphoses des Mangas."* YouTube, 16 Apr. 2018, www.youtube.com/watch?v=dpMVLK6aXDQ.

Super Eyepatch Wolf. *"The Impact of Akira: The Film That Changed Everything.* YouTube, 5 May 2018, www.youtube.com/watch?v=IqVoEpRIaKg.

VICE Japan. *"LIVING ON THE EDGE: 時を翔る暴走族　過去・現在・未来."* YouTube, 2 Sept. 2015, www.youtube.com/watch?v=W-GATxfUq00&t=32s.

Yanagimachi, Mitsuo. *God Speed You! Black Emperor*, 1976.

THE IMPACT OF
AKIRA
A MANGA
[R]EVOLUTION

Acknowledgments

- I would like to thank: Third Éditions for their confidence and ability to awaken the hidden potential of each of their collaborators (a trait undoubtedly acquired during their stay on Namek).

- My parents, my brother, and my grandmothers, for reminding me that I'm lucky enough to have that which is essential.

- Christelle for her lessons in courage.

- Léonie and Aurore for everything we share.

- Marie, for simply being herself.

- And Naïs for her enthusiasm.

Also available from Third Éditions:

Legal submission: November 2020
Printed in the European Union by Grafo.